THE LAVENDER GARDEN

the Lavender garden

BEAUTIFUL VARIETIES TO GROW AND GATHER

by ROBERT KOURIK

photographs by DEBORAH JONES

CHRONICLE BOOKS

SAN FRANCISCO

DEDICATED TO *John "Jack" Kourik*

While he probably won't eat many of the dishes in the cooking chapter, my Dad has always supported my work as a writer. I'm very grateful for his friendly comfort and encouragement over the years. Thanks.

LIBRARY OF CONGRESS CATALOGING-IN-PUBLICATION DATA AVAILABLE.

ISBN 0-8118-1570-6

PRINTED IN HONG KONG

BOOK AND COVER DESIGN BY JILL JACOBSON

THE PHOTOGRAPHER WISHES TO THANK: BEST PHOTO ASSISTANT, JERI JONES;

PROP STYLIST, AMY NATHAN; FOOD STYLISTS, AMY NATHAN AND NAN BULLOCK; CALIFORNIA NURSERIES

EMERISA GARDENS, SANTA ROSA; WESTERN HILLS, OCCIDENTAL; CALIFORNIA FLORA, FULTON.

LOCATIONS AND GARDENS GENEROUSLY PROVIDED BY THE GARDENER, BERKELEY;

LOUISE AND RON MANN, TERRE BLEUE, SONOMA; MATANZAS CREEK WINERY, SANTA ROSA;

STAR ROUTE FARMS, BOLINAS; BONNY DOON FARMS, AMERICA'S ORIGINAL ENGLISH LAVENDER ESTATE, SANTA CRUZ.

DISTRIBUTED IN CANADA BY RAINCOAST BOOKS • 8680 CAMBIE STREET • VANCOUVER, B.C. V6P 6M9

2 4 6 8 10 9 7 5 3 1

CHRONICLE BOOKS • 85 SECOND STREET • SAN FRANCISCO, CA 94105

WEB SITE: WWW.CHRONBOOKS.COM

contents

"with immediacy and intensity,
smell activates memory,
allowing our minds to travel freely in time."

TOM ROBBINS • *Jitterbug Perfume* 1984

evocative.   aromatic.

nostalgic.

romantic.

soothing.

healing.

All these words have been used to describe the fragrance of lavender.
Your first sniff of lavender may have been from the sweetly scented soap
your mother used or from a floral perfume or bath oil infused with that
unmistakable lavender essence. It is an aroma simultaneously fresh,
floral, sweet, pungent, haylike, woodsy, piny and reminiscent of citrus,
with perhaps an elusive hint of mint. Gardeners know the surprise and
pleasure of accidentally brushing up against feathery lavender foliage on
a warm day and releasing an invisible cloud of scent laden with the stuff
of dreams and memories.

The unique scent of this quintessential woody shrub is almost universally recognized, and lavender has been planted, tended, used, and cherished almost from the beginning of recorded civilization. The ancient Egyptians reputedly utilized lavender in their mummification processes and constructed stills to extract its essential oil. The Phoenicians and the peoples of early Arabia may have perfumed themselves with the plant's distinctive scent. Citizens of the Roman Empire routinely used lavender in perfumed oils, for bathing, for cooking, and to freshen the air. Throughout history the herb has also been employed as a general mind or mood "tonic," to repel insects and moths, for smoking pleasure in herbal blends, and even as an ingredient in witchcraft.

It is often stated that the English word *lavender* comes from the Latin *lavare*, "to wash," and that the Roman use of the herb brought about its usage in the laundry and linen drawers. However, it is not known whether lavender was brought to England by the Roman conquerors or by European traders. One of England's lavender aficionados, Sally Festing, makes a strong case that the word *lavender* most certainly did not come from *lavare* but from the earliest spelled form *livendula*—Latin for "livid" or "bluish."

In spite of over 2,500 years of recorded use, the origins of lavender are shrouded in mystery. Some varieties of the plant are thought to have first been domesticated in Arabia. The plant may then have traveled with Greek traders of around 600 BC to what are now the Hyères Islands off the southern coast of France, from whence it spread to the areas now known as France, Italy, and Spain. Lavender's first recorded arrival on the North American continent was with English pilgrims in the early 1600s. Just before this time, a sweet-smelling lavender was introduced commercially into England. What is now so commonly called English lavender did not originate in England, but the association continues.

Even though growing lavender has diminished in England since nearly the turn of the century, England continues to have the reputation for producing some of the world's sweetest lavender oils. Of course, the Provence region of France is still famous for its production of various types of essential lavender oil—from sweet oils for fragrances to bold, camphoric oils used to scent detergents.

Medieval and Renaissance laundry women were known as "lavenders," because they placed, much as we do today, sprigs or sachets of lavender flowers between layers of stored linens or dried cloths draped over lavender shrubs. Over the centuries, this aromatic plant has also been used therapeutically in soothing washes and baths, dabbed on fevered brows as a calming agent, and inhaled to relieve headaches and dizziness. Its healing properties have long held an honored place in herbal medicine.

Lavender's unique fragrance, emitted by a complex oil with over 180 different constituents and unduplicated by the chemistry of any other plant, has long been a staple of the perfume industry. The ideal perfume needs a balanced combination of a "top note," a "middle note," and a "bottom note." In this hierarchy, lavender is most often used as a top or middle note, lending a green, haylike sweetness along with what are known to perfume chemists as "fruity aspects."

To the romantic, however, no chemistry is required. The scent of lavender has long been associated with sweethearts and their ardor, and its effect on the libido, it turns out, is not merely wishful thinking. A scientific study by a Chicago research foundation revealed that the most arousing of all fragrances tested on its male subjects was, surprisingly, neither musk nor rose but a combination of the scents of lavender and pumpkin.

The essential oils found in the lavender plant's stems, leaves, and flowers are the source of its distinctive and evocative scent, and lavender oil of various types usually, depending upon the year, ranks fourth in quantity of all essential oils produced in the world. Each species of lavender contains a different range of oils, offering a unique flavor and aroma—some bold and untamed, others sweet and delicate. Body heat, hot water, a hot, moist, or foggy day, a hearty breeze, a forceful rain, or torrid air—all of these may induce lavender's essential oils to escape their biological receptacles and dissipate into the air to work subtle magic on our senses.

Lavender remains among the most versatile of all herbs: its foliage, stems, flowers, and seeds, alone or in combination, have a multiplicity of uses. To broadcast lavender's scent through our homes and lives, we employ candles, herb pillows, diffusers, flower wands, bouquets, sachets, soaps, wreaths, incense, and potpourris. We use the constituents of lavender to create perfumes, tinctures, bath oils, and shampoos, and even bring them into our kitchens as a seasoning for aromatic vinegars and marinades, a flavor for conserves, liqueurs, and jellies, and an ingredient in ice creams, sherbets, and baked goods, and to make candied blossoms to decorate wedding cakes and other desserts. Lavender oil is even one of the possible constituents of cigarette tobacco.

Lavender's reputation in herbal lore has been validated by modern medicine. Constituents of lavender oil have been shown to be effective against hyperactivity, insomnia, flatulence, bacteria, fungus, microbial activity on gums, airborne molds, and (when mixed with pine, thyme, mint, rosemary, clove, and cinnamon oils) the bacterium *Staphylococcus*, which can cause boils and infections. For medicinal use, essential oil of lavender is inhaled in steam, applied directly to the skin, or stirred into a relaxing warm bath. The foliage and flowers may be used as a tea or a poultice. Science is looking at lavender as an original source of compounds that could kill cancer cells and have been shown to reduce the size of breast cancer tumors in mice. Studies are under way to investigate the benefits of these natural cancer-fighting compounds on women.

And, of course, lavender is a garden plant par excellence, needing little in the way of water or fertilizer to produce a display of unique green, silvery, or blue-green foliage with fragrant flowers ranging from sky blue to lemon yellow to dark violet and lavender.

In this book you will learn how to make this remarkable plant part of your life—how to select from its many varieties, cultivate it in your garden, and put it to use in dozens of recipes and enchanting handicrafts. In doing so, you will be joining a fragrant tradition that spans millennia—the celebration and use of luscious, lovely lavender.

"here's your sweet lavender,
  sixteen sprigs a penny,
that you'll find my ladies,
  will smell as sweet as any."

LAVENDER SELLER'S CRY • *London, England* CA. 1900

the botany of Lavender

Lavender belongs to the large plant family of mints, a botanical grouping distinguished by square stems and, in many cases, remarkable fragrances. Its "cousins" include culinary and herbal tea mints, ornamental and cooking sages, marjorams, thymes, and horehounds. Not all lavender shrubs are highly scented; some varieties are lovely garden specimens, but have little fragrance. Others are insignificant to look at but are rich in aroma.

Lavenders present the gardener with many choices. With over 15 species of lavender, there are plenty of types to choose from. One species, the English lavender, tops the list with over 40 named varieties available by mail-order catalog alone. From this offering of named English lavenders, you can choose many shades of flowers from the purest white to pale pink to clear violet-blue to dark purple. The only lavender with yellow-green blossoms (*Lavandula viridis*) has no named selections—only its species.

As evergreen shrubs, lavender also offers the gardener a wide assortment of form and foliage color. The smallest English lavenders can be sheared to tight herbal hedges only 6 to 12 inches tall and wide. As is commonly seen in etchings of herbal gardens in medieval Europe, these compact forms of lavender were and remain quite popular as edging plants. Other lavenders grow to 4 or more feet tall and even wider. Lavender also comes in every size in between. The choice of sizes means you can select a lavender plant to act as a ground cover, a small shrub, or a medium shrub. And these are not slow-growing plants. Lavender shrubs fill in nicely within a year or two—depending upon how far apart they are planted.

Almost every size comes in a form with evergreen foliage that ranges from a dusty green to a silvery gray. Lavender is famous for its silver or gray tomentose—hairy—leaves and lends itself to a prominent spot in the silver-gray perennial border or as a plant to high-light dark green areas of the garden. A few species of lavenders have bright green, chartreuse leaves. Lavender leaves range from long and narrow, simple, and coniferlike to lacy, fernlike, and ornate. There is a leaf pattern to fit nearly every style of garden.

Lavenders do not live as long as most woody shrubs. Some specimens still look healthy and vigorous after 10 years, but most begin to decline before that time. Fortunately, lavenders are easy to buy, simple to plant, and reach mature size rather quickly.

To distinguish among the many lavender varieties and choose the right ones for your needs, you'll need to know both the common name and the botanical name for each lavender. The common name of a plant is usually written in English—for example, "forget-me-not" or "Spanish lavender"—but since these common names often come from folk culture and can be misleading, botanical science relies on a formal system of names, or nomenclature, to distinguish one plant from another. Botanists, along with many nursery keepers and gardeners, use Latin terms inherited from the medieval origins of botanical classification to distinguish plants. In this book, all of the scientific (Latin) names are italicized.

In botanical nomenclature, every plant has, in addition to its common name, a name composed of its genus and species. The genus, which always comes first and is spelled with a capital letter, identifies a large grouping of plants with shared characteristics, including a similar type of flower. All lavenders, for example, belong to the genus *Lavandula*. The species name, which always follows the genus and is not capitalized, identifies a specific member of the genus. For example, the lavender known by the common name English lavender is properly labeled *Lavandula angustifolia*. The descriptive species word *angustifolia* means "narrow-leaved."

When appropriate, a plant's botanical name includes a variety name. A variety is like a subdivision of a species due to naturally occurring or selectively bred populations or plants that differ from the species in minor characteristics. Varieties are selected from natural seedling mutations and are always propagated from cuttings taken from the mutations rather than from seeds. The variety name follows the species label and is usually preceded by the abbreviation "var." For example, there is a French lavender, *Lavandula dentata*, that is formally labeled *Lavandula dentata* var. *candicans*. This variety produces a dusty, silver-gray foliage that appears quite different from the typical bright to rich green foliage of French lavender.

Sometimes botanists add a subspecies name. Technically, a subspecies is a plant that occurs naturally in a geographically different place than the general species. To designate a subspecies, the abbreviation "ssp." or "subsp." precedes the assigned Latin label, for example, *Lavandula stoechas* ssp. *pendunculata*. The pendunculata lavenders originated in

Spain, Portugal, North Africa, the Balkans, and Asia Minor. The species, *L. stoechas*, comes only from the mountains of France, Spain, and Portugal, and from what were formerly known as the Stoechades Islands off the coast of France (now called the Hyères Islands).

In this book, after a *Lavandula* is mentioned once in each new chapter, it is written thereafter as *L.* followed by the species.

When you go to buy a lavender plant, be aware that you may encounter confusing terms. A species lavender, as opposed to the species of a lavender, is a plant that has all the general characteristics of the species. If the plants have been grown from seed, however, there may be slight variations between them due to natural genetic variability. As with human beings, these offspring may greatly resemble the parent or look radically different. A species lavender may also be grown from cuttings; in this case, each plant will be identical to the mother plant, the plant from which the cuttings were taken. In this case, the mother plant of a species lavender is simply another species plant and is not chosen for any specific or distinctive characteristics.

A more important designation to identify when shopping for a lavender is the term *cultivar*. A cultivar, also called a named cultivar or selection, is a specimen of a plant variety especially selected from seedlings because it differs uniquely from the "normal" species plant. For example, if the seed of a violet-flowering species of lavender should happen to produce a white-flowering plant, a cultivar name can be given to this special chance seedling. Nature makes the new plant, but a person selects it from all of the variable species seedlings. For this reason a cultivar is also known as a selection. To maintain the white flower color, or any other distinctive attributes, of this newly discovered seedling, it must be propagated only from cuttings. This vegetative propagation, as it is known, ensures that all the young cultivar plants have traits identical to those of the original chance seedling.

The cultivar name appears after the genus and species names and is distinguished by single quotes. For example, 'Munstead' is a cultivar of the English lavender species *L. angustifolia*, and any full written reference to it should include its genus, species, and cultivar name—*Lavandula angustifolia* 'Munstead'. However, as is customary, after the first reference in chapter, cultivar names are abbreviated, for example, *L. a.* 'Munstead', or simply 'Munstead'.

calyxes ENGLISH LAVENDER

bracts SPANISH LAVENDER

corollas FRENCH LAVENDER

calyxes

bracts

corollas

In order to enjoy and cook with lavender, it's helpful to know a little about lavender's fragrant anatomy. Each lavender flower head is composed of many different parts. Discerning some of the major parts brings more appreciation to the cultivation of lavender. By distinguishing the sweet-tasting corollas (petals) from the harsher-flavored calyxes (the bases) of the flowers, you can select the sweetest parts of the plant to cook with. Also, the most dramatic part of a blooming Spanish lavender is not the petals, but the colorful upright flags or wings—more properly called the bracts. These bracts are tasteless for cooking purposes.

Each lavender stem is crested with a flower head, also called an inflorescence. Images on the facing page show the major parts of a flower head. Botanists, being compulsive labelers, have many more names for all of the many minute protrusions and crannies of a lavender bloom, but these illustrations include only the most important components—the ones that gardeners see and smell.

In all types of lavender, each flower bud is composed of two major parts, the calyx and the corolla. Both are a source of some of the aromatic oils responsible for lavender's mesmerizing scent.

The base of each calyx is attached to the flower stem. The calyx is tubular in shape and can be slightly hairy or nearly smooth (as with English lavenders) or quite rough and woolly (as with French lavender). The flower emerges from the open end of the tubular calyx, which may, as with French lavender, end in a hoodlike shape.

The corolla is slightly trumpet shaped and tubular, with five lobes. The corollas open randomly: portions of each whorl bloom, while other parts remain as hollow or seed-filled calyxes—although they start to bloom near the bottom of the flower heads.

The Spanish lavenders have a unique feature on top of their flower heads—showy, richly colored bracts, often called wings, rabbit ears, or flags in honor of their ornamental prominence. Because the true blossoms (corollas) of these plants are small, the flashy, deep purple or dark violet bracts, actually leaflike formations, are often mistaken for petals. The less showy pale mauve bracts of French lavender protrude only slightly above the flower head, and are cupped together more like praying hands.

CHAPTER 2

"There's flowers for you:
Hot lavender, mints, savory, marjoram:
The marigold, that goes to bed wi' the sun,
And with him rises weeping; these are flowers
Of middle summer, and I think they are given
To men of middle age."

WILLIAM SHAKESPEARE • *The Winter's Tale*

choosing a Lavender

This piquant and versatile garden plant provides both ornamental foliage and colorful bloom in a variety of North American climates. Ample drifts of lavender rambling over berms and across large areas make a stunning feature in any landscape. Shrubs may also be laid out in a formal pattern, such as a knot garden, or planted row on row. When in bloom, a small regimented field with parallel ranks of lavender is a glorious treat for the eyes and nose. For an even more dramatic effect, these parallel rows may be planted at an odd angle to the perimeter. More uses for annual and perennial lavenders are described in detail under the discussion of each species, variety, and cultivar.

The time when lavenders bloom in your garden depends on the varieties you plant, your location, annual weather patterns, and microclimates, which can shift the normal season of bloom by at least one week in an early or late direction. In some favorable climates such as northern Virginia's Zone 7, you can plant for a bloom period that lasts from some time in June until late September. In the most moderate, truly Mediterranean climates, such as the San Francisco Bay Area's Zone 9, you'll be able to have at least one kind of lavender blooming every day of the year. The description of each species and cultivar of lavender in this chapter includes a mention of its period of typical bloom.

Lavender is a tried-and-true shrub for planting where deer roam. Although these beautiful but destructive creatures, especially young fawns, occasionally sample individual flower heads, they generally eat so few blossoms that their absence is seldom noted, and they rarely eat lavender foliage. However, like any other plant, lavender can be damaged by large animals walking or lying on it.

Lavenders can be found thriving, albeit with a little help, in planting Zones 5 through 11, as based on the USDA Hardiness Zone Map (see page 116). Whatever the planting zone, all lavenders are sensitive to microclimates—the subtle differences of sun, wind, rain, drainage, humidity, and temperature found in our homes and backyards.

Gardeners in California's dry-summer-region (Zones 9 and 10) will have a much easier time growing lavenders than will gardeners in the humidity and summer rain of Florida (Zones 8 through 10). Too much humidity can cause mildew or fungus to form on the foliage and too much rain can promote root rot, so in humid, rainy areas, lavenders will suffer unless grown in large well-drained containers placed in an area sheltered from summer rains. Locating a potted lavender under an eave on the west- or south-facing side of a house or deck will often help keep it drier than if it were in the surrounding garden.

In cold-winter climates, favorite potted lavenders are often moved indoors to escape frostbite and then are set out again in the spring. Ambitious gardeners in these areas take their container-grown lavenders inside before the first fall frost, moving the pots or planters to a basement or indoor room that is certain to stay above 32° F. Cold-weather quarters for lavender must also be equipped with plenty of lighting to keep the foliage healthy through the winter.

Listed with each of the following species of lavenders is a correct common name and botanical name. Any other name or names often used in place of the proper name are listed in parentheses. These alternate names, although improper, have often been used synonymously for the accurate names and are called synonymies. For example, English lavender is the agreed-upon common name. But some people or mail-order catalogs still use the older, less precise name *true lavender*, the name given in parentheses. In this example, the only correct botanical name is *Lavandula angustifolia*. In parentheses are *L. officinalis, L. angustifolius, L. vera, L. spica, L. pyrenaica,* and *L. delphinensis*—all synonymies for *L. angustifolia*.

English Lavender

English lavender is the most popular garden lavender in North America. Despite the name, English lavender is thought to have originally grown in stony, dry, alkaline soils at altitudes between 2,100 and 6,000 feet in the southern French Alps. Some historians maintain that this fragrant shrub arrived on British shores with the Romans; others believe that it appeared in the early 1300s. *Lavandula angustifolia* is associated with England because this species was the backbone of England's original lavender-oil industry in the late 1700s.

Although the correct botanical name of English lavender is *L. angustifolia*, it has been and may be sold or labeled as *L. officinalis* and *L. vera*. *Officinalis* is a reference to all medicinal plants and plants from which we derive essential oils; *vera* means "true." To this day, some catalogs and nurseries still sell *L. officinalis* or *L. vera* as "true" lavender or *L. angustifolia*.

COMMON NAME   English lavender (also sold as true lavender).

BOTANICAL NAME   *Lavandula angustifolia* (*L. officinalis, L. angustifolius, L. vera, L. spica, L. pyrenaica, L. delphinensis*; this last species has longer, thinner flower heads than *L. angustifolia* but is still considered the same species as *L. angustifolia*).

FLOWER DESCRIPTION   Thin, squarish stems rise 6 to 12 inches above the foliage to support flower heads. Tapered flower heads usually extend 1 or more inches along the stem and are much longer than their widths.

Whatever its shape, the average English lavender flower head shows six to ten whorls of flower buds stretched along the stem beneath the main head. Half-inch-long trumpet-shaped corollas, when in bloom, protrude from the calyx of each bud. The calyx appears as stiff brownish or greenish tissue enveloping the bottom of each corolla. Individual corollas open randomly over the entire flower head, not in sequence.

The corollas may be colored mauve, blue-violet, violet shading to light blue, pale purple, bluish mauve, modest purple, or rich violet.

BLOOM PERIOD   Once in June; mid- to late May through early June in Zone 7.

PLANT AND FOLIAGE DESCRIPTION   Small shrub that typically grows 2 to 3 feet in both height and width, with the foliage naturally forming an irregular half-dome. Left uncut, the plant may become somewhat rangy, and rain, irrigation, or snow may cause the branches to fall open. Because of this tendency, English lavender is frequently sheared into a tighter, more dense version of its natural shape. It is also sometimes clipped to form small rectangular edgings for formal gardens or herbal knot gardens.

The leaves of this lavender are narrow, lance shaped, and up to nearly 2 inches long. They range in color from pale olive green to the more characteristic blue-green or glaucous (having a whitish, grayish, or pale bluish powdery covering on the leaves).

HARDINESS AND PLANTING RANGE   The hardiest of all lavender species. Rated hardy from Zone 5 (with winter temperatures to -20° to -10° F) through Zone 11. Can be grown in places listed on the USDA map as colder than Zone 5 if the right microclimate is chosen. The lower limit is about -25° F.

TYPICAL LANDSCAPE USE   Common plant for edging annual flower, perennial flower, vegetable, and herb beds. Foliage can be allowed to grow unrestrained, with just a single firm clipping after each season's bloom. Regular clipping will keep the plant in any desired form, but will reduce it to primarily a foliage accent, with few blooms. Frequently used in traditional European formal gardens such as herbal knot gardens, potagers, and parterres (European ornate floral bed designs with low clipped hedges). English lavender, like rosemary or privets, can be trained in topiary shapes, although this is seldom done these days.

CULINARY USE   This sweetest smelling and flavored of all lavenders can be used for all recipes that call for lavender flowers or foliage. The delicate flavor of the blossoms is a marvelous addition to ice cream, sorbets, baked desserts, and candied-flower assortments.

SPECIAL USES/COMMENTS   One of the primary sources of essential oils for perfume use. Also proven as an insecticide against aphids and a repellent of cockroaches.

A fungal disease called shab (See Chapter 3) devastated the English crop of *L. angustifolia* in the 1960s but doesn't appear to be a problem in North America.

Favorite English Lavender Cultivars

The various cultivars of English lavender can be divided into four categories, based on flower color.

WHITE-FLOWERING CULTIVARS
'Alba'
'Dwarf White'
'Nana Alba'
L. a. compacta 'Alba'

PINK-FLOWERING CULTIVARS
'English Pink'
'Hidcote Pink'
> *Differs, according to Dr. Arthur O. Tucker, recognized as the best authority on* Lavandula *nomenclature in North America, only slightly from* 'Jean Davis', 'Rosea', *and* 'Lodden Pink' *(from Tommy Carlisle's Nursery at Twyford in Berkshire, England), but the essential oil of all of these plants is the same. Along with* 'Hidcote', *perhaps one of the hardiest of all English lavenders.*

DARK VIOLET-FLOWERING CULTIVARS
'Dwarf Blue'
'Hidcote'
'Lodden Blue'
'Martha Roedrick'
'Mitcham Grey'
> *Greatly resembles* 'Hidcote'.

'Munstead'
'Nana Atropurpurea'
> *Very similar to* 'Hidcote' *and may be the parent plant for* 'Hidcote', 'Mitcham Grey', *and* 'Loddon Blue'.

'Tucker's Early Purple'

Introduced by Thomas De Baggio of Earthworks, Arlington, Virginia.

'W. K. Doyle' ('Dark Supreme')

'W. K. Doyle' named for the father-in-law of Thomas DeBaggio and husband of Irene Doyle. See blue-flowering cultivars, below.

BLUE-FLOWERING CULTIVARS

'Graves'

'Gray Lady'

'Irene Doyle'

Also called 'Two Seasons' because it has two distinct flowering seasons; introduced in 1983 by Thomas DeBaggio.

'Maillette'

'Twickle Purple'

From Twickle Castle, Holland. Also labeled as 'Nana Compacta' or 'Compacta' (both often sold in North America as 'Munstead'). True 'Twickle Purple' is probably quite rare and may be the same as L. delphinensis.

This cultivar is thought to have originated as a selection by the famous English landscape designer Gertrude Jekyll at her home, Munstead Wood in Surrey, and to have been introduced by her to the garden trades in 1916. However, since Jekyll never mentions the plant in her many writings, some maintain that its true origin is a mystery.

Although 'Munstead' lavender is often sold as seed, it is somewhat misleading to sell seed for a named cultivar, or selection, since a true cultivar is propagated from cuttings, in order to ensure that the progeny exactly resemble the parent or mother plant. Expect some genetic variability with 'Munstead' seedlings. The true form of this plant is rather hard to come by due to how often it's grown from seed.

COMMON NAME 'Munstead' lavender.

BOTANICAL NAME *Lavandula angustifolia* 'Munstead'.

FLOWER DESCRIPTION A typical 'Munstead' flower has a dark aster-violet corolla, also described as bright deep lavender-blue, with a dark-violet calyx. The flower is a paler blue than that of the popular 'Hidcote' variety.

Dr. Arthur O. Tucker advises that what is sold as 'Munstead' and 'Dwarf Munstead' in the United States is not a 'Munstead' selection, but the weaker plant 'Compacta'. The true 'Munstead', according to Tucker, has a darker purple corolla.

BLOOM PERIOD By mid-June in most areas, ahead of *L. a.* 'Compacta', a lavender-blue flowering variety often sold as 'Munstead'. Mid- to late May through early June in Zone 7.

PLANT AND FOLIAGE DESCRIPTION The bush is small, semiprostrate and excellent as a border plant. The gray-green narrow-leaved foliage grows 6 to 8 inches in both height and width, with blossoms reaching 14 to 16 inches. Individual plants may grow irregularly and need one or two seasonal clippings for an even shape.

HARDINESS AND PLANTING RANGE Considered about as hardy as the species English lavender—Zones 5 through 8. It thrives in the formal gardens reestablished over the past decade by gardener Brigit Deeds at Shelburne Farms in Vermont on the shore of Lake Champlain. Although the surrounding area is rated as Zone 4 (-30° to -20° F), the lake moderates the climate for a short distance beyond its waters, and the microclimate is equal to Zone 5, which otherwise is located many miles away.

TYPICAL LANDSCAPE USE   Popular as a petite formal or informal edging plant for flower borders, potagers, herbal knot gardens, Victorian cottage gardens, and parterres. Can be clipped to just about any shape and may be used for small topiaries. Can be grown individually in small terra-cotta pots or grouped in a large container.

CULINARY USE   Use the foliage and flowers as you would those of any species of English lavender. The flowers contribute a distinctive rich violet color to fruit salads, mixed green salads, and candied blossoms for decoration. The foliage is much more strongly flavored than the blooms and should be used with caution. Care should be also taken when harvesting foliage from this plant, as taking too much will greatly affect its form.

'LAVENDER LADY'

This remarkable selection blooms in its first summer from spring-sown seed. The recently introduced cultivar (an All-America Selection in 1994) now makes it possible to grow lavender shrubs outdoors in climates where it's normally too cold for them to survive the winter. Remember, however, that a true cultivar is propagated vegetatively, and as with 'Munstead', expect some genetic variability with 'Lavender Lady' seedlings. This plant is probably a selection of a 'Munstead' seedling.

COMMON NAME 'Lavender Lady'.

BOTANICAL NAME *Lavandula angustifolia* 'Lavender Lady'.

FLOWER DESCRIPTION   Tall flower stalks rise 4 to 5 inches above the foliage and resemble a loose form of the *L. angustifolia* bloom, with deep lavender corollas. Prized for its ability to repeat bloom, in flushes, over much of the summer.

BLOOM PERIOD   At least from July into August in New England. In flushes from early June through September, at the minimum, in northern California. Mid- to late May through early June in Zone 7.

PLANT AND FOLIAGE DESCRIPTION   Archetypal gray-green lavender foliage that grows to form a petite mound 8 to 12 inches tall.

HARDINESS AND PLANTING RANGE Can be grown anywhere in North America if seed is started indoors and the seedlings are set out after the danger of frost is over. Blooms well before the first hard frosts of fall arrive to kill the plant. In warm-winter areas, Zones 7 through 11, it will become established as a perennial.

TYPICAL LANDSCAPE USE Excellent plant for single plantings in small pieces of ornamental pottery or for mass plantings in large, well-drained containers. Wonderful border plant for many garden styles and especially attractive in Italian, Spanish, French provincial, and Mediterranean designs. May also be used in herbal knot gardens, European potagers, or modern ornamental Xeriscapes (low-water-use plantings).

CULINARY USE Use as you would any species or cultivar form of English lavender.

SPECIAL USES/COMMENTS Sow plenty of extra seed, as germination isn't reliable. Some gardeners, instead of trying to germinate seed, prefer to take cuttings at the end of the season to winter over indoors. With some resolve on the part of the gardener, 'Lavender Lady' extends the cultivation of lavender to just about anywhere.

LEFT TO RIGHT:

*Lavandula
stoechas,*
a species form
of Spanish
lavender

*Lavandula
stoechas* ssp.
pendunculata
'Otto Quast',
a cultivar of
Spanish
lavender

*Lavandula
stoechas* ssp.
pendunculata
'Atlas',
a cultivar of
Spanish
lavender

Spanish Lavender

A plant resembling what is now known as Spanish lavender was described by Greek botanist Pedanios Dioscorides in the first century AD as "a small branching bush with thin numerous leaves, the flowers of a purple color gathered at the head of the stalk." Dioscorides noted that the plant, which he assumed was native to what are now called the Hyères Islands off the coast of France, was used medicinally. In 1656 John Tradescant the Elder, a botanist living near London, England, published a catalog of his massive plant collection, which listed "Stæchas, Cassidony or French Lavender." This type of lavender produced the most commonly distilled oil in the Middle Ages. Since that time and for reasons now lost, *L. stoechas* has come to be known as Spanish lavender and has enjoyed an important herbal, medicinal, and ornamental place in home gardens. Although this type of lavender no longer plays a significant role in the production of commercial lavender oil, it is ideal for making potpourris and sachets, for seasoning meats grilled over hardwood charcoal, and for using in floral arrangements.

COMMON NAME   Spanish lavender (also sold as French lavender or Italian lavender).

BOTANICAL NAME   *Lavandula stoechas.*

FLOWER DESCRIPTION   Dioscorides' reference to those telltale purple-topped stalks surely describes what we now more properly call bracts, which although showy, are not true petals but a type of leaf formation. Each flower head is tipped with an indigo-purple ribbon-bow topknot of bracts that resembles a glorious fluttering flame. The bracts of all species of Spanish lavender are much larger than the corollas along the flower head, and those of some *stoechas* cultivars, like *L. s.* ssp. *pendunculata* (also labeled and called 'Otto Quast', 'Otto Quastii', or 'Quastii'), grow up to ¾ inch in length above the flower head. The bracts of the species form are ⅛ to ½ inch tall.

The flower heads resemble miniature pineapples, with small purplish black flowers that open all over the flower head. There are little orange-gold "eyes" (the gold is actually a spot of pollen) arranged in four rows like little corn cobs along the length of the flower head.

BLOOM PERIOD   Profusely in most climates in early summer, somewhat overlapping the blooming period of English lavender. In many areas, especially those with mild summers and winters, an early rush of bloom occurs in midspring, bloom in early summer, and another flush of color in fall. Occasional blossoms can be found almost every month, except during the dead of winter, in temperate-winter areas. Plants grown indoors or in a greenhouse bloom year-round. Rain or sprinkler irrigation will knock over many or most flower stalks on this type of lavender, due to the weight of the moisture on bracts and flower heads. Be sure to prune back hard after peak summer bloom to encourage shorter and sturdier flower stems.

PLANT AND FOLIAGE DESCRIPTION   Typically grows 12 to 18 inches tall, with seedlings occasionally reaching 22 to 24 inches, and often somewhat wider than the height. Leaves are long and pointed, somewhat resembling those of rosemary *(Rosmarinus officinalis)* foliage, and are a soft gray-green with a slightly rolled-over edge. The diminutive foliage makes an interesting contrast with the abundance of bloom.

HARDINESS AND PLANTING RANGE   Far less hardy than the benchmark English species. While English lavender can tolerate, under the best of conditions, temperatures down to -25° F, Spanish lavender is only reliably hardy to about 20° F, a range corresponding roughly to Zones 9 through 11. In my northern California garden, a 10 year low, three nights when the temperature dropped to about 15° F during a moist period, froze back most of my Spanish lavenders to the ground, although some plants regrew from the crown of the roots. Some catalogs rate Spanish lavender down to 5° F. The drier the air during a cold spell, the greater the damage potential to lavenders.

TYPICAL LANDSCAPE USE   In areas with congenial climates for its growth, Spanish lavender is most commonly used as a mass planting for the middle ground of a border or landscape planting, with taller shrubs behind and low-growing plants in the foreground. It can also be used as a ground cover. In addition, this tightly knit shrub can be planted as an informal, somewhat spherical hedge or clipped tightly into a formal topiary or hedge shape. It is also a good plant for indoor culture and thrives in large pots—terra-cotta pottery for a look especially reminiscent of the lavender regions of the Mediterranean. Tolerates more acid soils than English lavenders.

CULINARY USE   Unfortunately, the bracts are all show and no flavor. While the flower heads do contain some lavender fragrance, they are too large and woody to use in ordinary cuisine. The flower heads and bracts, however, can be candied—for ornamental purposes only—to make a dramatic cake decoration.

The foliage holds an aroma similar to that of English lavender but somewhat more robust, with hints of more pungent essential oils like mint, camphor, rosemary, pine, and citrus. Although the scent of Spanish lavender is a bit more medicinal than that of typical English lavender, the cooked or grilled foliage has little medicinal taste and stands up well to game, red meat, and other hardy dishes; it may also be used in herb breads. This is neither the foliage nor the flower of choice for sweet desserts, ice cream, or sorbet.

SPECIAL USES/COMMENTS   An active component in Spanish lavender is the compound fenchone, which contributes a fresh piny tang, camphoric elements, and sweet lime scents. Fenchone is used to provide a lift in low-priced soap, bath preparations, and room sprays and to mask odors. Spanish lavender yields more oil per acre harvested than English varieties. For a more stately and refined look in the garden, try planting *L. stoechas* 'Alba'. This Spanish lavender produces pure white bracts that are glorious during a full moon.

SPANISH LAVENDER 'ATLAS'

COMMON NAME   Spanish lavender 'Atlas' (Pendunculata lavender 'Atlas').

BOTANICAL NAME   *Lavandula stoechas* ssp. *pendunculata* 'Atlas' (*L. pendunculata* 'Atlas' or *L. stoechas* 'Atlas').

FLOWER DESCRIPTION   Truly spectacular bracts, of the same rich indigo-purple as those of a typical seedling Spanish lavender, but towering up to 2 inches above the large pineapplelike flower head. This plant provides a very dramatic presentation in the garden if rain or sprinklers don't cause the bracts and flower stems to collapse. Also sports little orange-gold "eyes" along the flower's length and small purplish black flowers opening randomly all over the flower head.

BLOOM PERIOD   Similar to the summer flush of bloom obtained with regular Spanish lavender, but doesn't bloom during the winter in mild climates. If pruned back firmly after the summer bloom, this lavender will produce another flush of flowers in late summer, although perhaps fewer and less colorful blooms. Plants grown indoors or in a greenhouse bloom year-round.

PLANT AND FOLIAGE DESCRIPTION   Soft gray-green foliage similar to that of the unnamed Spanish lavender species. Leaves longer and shrub more vigorous—up to 2 feet tall and wide.

HARDINESS AND PLANTING RANGE   Probably the same as that of the species form. 'Atlas' has tolerated temperatures down to 15° F in my garden.

TYPICAL LANDSCAPE USE   This is a shrub worth using as an accent plant—a single plant placed against a neutral backdrop to display its unique beauty—in a flower border or ornamental shrub planting. In any case, it should be sited where its impressive bracts can easily be inspected at close range. If 'Atlas' is situated so that the flowers are illuminated by the afternoon sun, the flags will glow like stained-glass windows; the towering bracts also look striking against an earth- or terra-cotta-colored wall. A number of the plants can be massed together, but only where rain or irrigation isn't likely to dash the blossoms to the ground. Suited only to the largest terra-cotta pottery (24 inches in diameter or greater).

CULINARY USE As with many Spanish lavenders, the aroma and flavor of 'Atlas' are like those of English lavender, but with minty, camphoric, rosemarylike, piny, and citronlike overtones. The foliage is aromatic, but not as sweet as that of the lavenders typically used for perfume and bath products. Good for grilling, this shrub produces so much foliage that surplus clippings can be used to smoke meats, fish, and vegetables. Like those of species Spanish lavenders, the heads, though large and beautiful, are woody, and the bracts have no particular flavor, so candied blossoms are useful only for decoration.

SPECIAL USES/COMMENTS Sets some viable seed and produces seedlings in the surrounding mulch, though such seedlings are usually oddly colored and much less ornamental than the named variety grown from cuttings. Appears to cross with the species Spanish lavender and with *L. viridis*.

GREEN LAVENDER

This plant is technically a different species from the true *L. stoechas*, though the flower is so similar in shape (though *not* in color) to the flower of the typical Spanish lavender that, for the average gardener, it easily fits into this category, and some catalogs list it as a variety of *L. stoechas*. Baron Frederic Charles Jean de Gingins, in his 1826 *Natural History of the Lavenders*, states that this lavender comes from a "very small area of Portugal along the banks of the Tagus river, and in Madeira."

COMMON NAME Green lavender (also sold as yellow lavender or green Spanish lavender).
BOTANICAL NAME *Lavandula viridis* (*L. stoechas* var. *viridis*, *L. virens*).
FLOWER DESCRIPTION Produces the same squarish pineapple-shaped flower head as

L. stoechas, but without the dark purple corollas and orange-gold "eyes." Instead, the heads are a lime-yellow green, with insignificant white or very pale creamy yellow corollas. The bracts are ½ to ¾ inch tall and a pure yellow lime. Although they fade quickly, especially in hot weather, many others open at the same time. Spent bracts, unless clipped, may cling to the head for weeks in a dull-brown withered state.

BLOOM PERIOD   Produces some blooms virtually all year in moderate-winter areas and nonstop bloom early to midsummer, although heat waves may reduce the number of blossoms. Plants grown indoors or in a greenhouse bloom year-round.

PLANT AND FOLIAGE DESCRIPTION   Produces bright chartreuse, nearly apple-green foliage up to 3 feet tall and equally wide. Amount of yellow in the foliage is close in color to that of the annual 'Bells of Ireland', but clearer and less muddy. The color is hard to work with in the garden, but also is fairly clean looking and distinctive. Green lavender requires pruning to maintain a dense, even canopy.

HARDINESS AND PLANTING RANGE   Not as hardy as *L. stoechas* or 'Atlas'. It froze back considerably at 15° F in my garden, but seedlings resprouted from the exposed mulch.

TYPICAL LANDSCAPE USE   Unusual color best reserved as a focal point or accent in a perennial flower border. Use sparingly, with a backdrop of rich green foliage. Nearby flowers should be planted with an eye to complementing the distinctive color of the foliage and blossoms with a range of pastel and clear yellows or neutral whites.

CULINARY USE   In my opinion, this is the best of all lavenders for grilling, herb breads, and hearty dishes. The foliage is wilder, "gamier," and more primitive than that of the typical Spanish or English lavenders, though it contains a combination of mint, camphor, rosemary, pine, and citrus fragrances and flavors similar to the Spanish lavender species form. Complicated herbal flavor of green lavender, however, is weighted more toward the rosemary and pine components. Some say this lavender tastes more undomesticated than all other lavender leaves; others say it's even sweeter than the conventional English lavenders. Judge for yourself, but don't pass this one up.

SPECIAL USES/COMMENTS   You get lots of free plants, as green lavender readily produces fertile seeds and appears to cross with all Spanish lavenders. When planted in groups, the seedlings closely resemble the parent *L. viridis* plants. A big hit at the 1995 Chelsea Garden Show in London, *L. viridis* is becoming the latest rage in English gardening.

*Lavandula
dentata,*
a species form
of French
lavender

*Lavandula
dentata* var.
candicans
'French Grey'

Lavandula
x *intermedia*
'Grosso',
a cultivar of
Lavandin

French Lavender

The Provence region of southeast France, renowned for its lavender, produced, as of 1993, about 992 tons of all types of lavender oil annually. Oddly enough, none of this oil came from the plant known in North America as French lavender, but from a cross between English lavender (*L. angustifolia*) and spike lavender (*L. latifolia*). The so-called lavandin oil (sometimes represented as French oil) harvested from this hybrid has a robust, more spirited, and less sweet flavor or scent than *L. angustifolia* oil. The correct generic name for lavandin (pronounced lah-vahn-deen) oil plants is *Lavandula* x *intermedia*—the x stands for "cross," meaning a hybrid plant.

Baron Frederic Charles Jean de Gingins, in his 1826 *Natural History of the Lavenders*, asserts that *L. dentée* (probably what we call French lavender, now known as *L. dentata*) originally came from "a territory between 36 and 38 degrees latitude in the Balearic Islands, and along the Tagus [river] in east-central Spain and West through all of Portugal, where it was cultivated in the time of Clusius." Carolus Clusius (Charles de Lecluse) was a Flemish botanist-physician, born in 1526.

The botanical species name *L. dentata* comes from the Latin *dentate*, meaning "toothed or edged with toothlike projections."

COMMON NAME French lavender (also sold as Spanish lavender, fringed lavender).

BOTANICAL NAME *Lavandula dentata*.

FLOWER DESCRIPTION Compact to fairly large flower heads (up to 2 inches tall by ½ inch wide), round (as opposed to the squared-off pineapple shape of *L. stoechas*), and decidedly tomentose (covered with densely matted hairs). Tiny corollas of the true flowers are a pale to medium rich violet and are less prominent than those of most other lavenders. Bracts at the top of each flower head, approximately ¼ inch wide and ½ inch long, are less dramatic than those of Spanish lavenders, but still quite showy as they reach up to form a layered peak and delicately fold back to display their color, resembling hands loosely folded in prayer or the layered "petals" of an opening artichoke. The marvelous color of the bracts is a slightly smoky, hazed purple variously described as pale blue-violet, vivid bluish violet, or mauve (a moderate grayish violet). While the tone of each flower head is pastel, so many blossoms often open at one time that the overall effect is quite dramatic.

BLOOM PERIOD In coastal gardens with moderate climates, virtually year-round. Periods of peak bloom occur in mid- to late winter, in spring, and again in early fall. In cold-weather climates (Zone 7), blooms only in the summer. Outside of the most benign winter climates, blooms year-round if kept in pots and brought indoors and outside at the appropriate times.

PLANT AND FOLIAGE DESCRIPTION Robust plant grows more than 3 feet tall and 4 or more feet wide—some individual plants with self-rooted stems over 6 feet wide. Foliage is composed of narrow, oblong leaves, about ⅓ inch wide and 1¼ inches long. Edges of each leaf are finely toothed with wavy margins and slightly rolled inward. The distinctively scalloped edge looks like the marks on a sandwich left by dental impressions. Color of foliage may vary with plant variety from shades of dark pine green to bright green to pastel grass green. All forms can have slightly grayish overtones and/or a slight fuzz. These variations are categorized botanically as either a tomentose (hairy) leaf or a glaucous leaf (pale grayish or bluish green, covered with a grayish, bluish, or whitish waxy coating, or bloom, that is easily rubbed off). Unlike the English varieties, *L. dentata* foliage can reach its mature size in as little as one season.

HARDINESS AND PLANTING RANGE Hardy to 15° F. This plant froze to the ground in my garden at 15° to 17° F, but rebounded from the base of the stems and crown of the root system.

TYPICAL LANDSCAPE USE This vigorous shrub can easily fill in the middle ground of a flower border. The long season of bloom in some climates makes *L. dentata* a good plant to use in quantity as a prevailing theme in a landscape planting or border.

Since this plant maintains a consistent, attractive foliage all year in moderate climates, it's a good choice for growing in front of tall annual bedding plants or perennials that die to the ground seasonally. Examples of seasonal perennials include artichokes, cardoon, bronze fennel, dahlias (although lavender doesn't need the fertility that dahlias require), and asters. Some tall bedding plants that look attractive behind French lavender are cosmos, blue-flowering salvias, bachelor's buttons, nicotiana, and larkspur. *L. dentata* flower heads and foliage also blend beautifully with pink-flowering morning glories or other clean, clear, soft pink blooms.

Plant may be grown in large movable containers where the winter climate is too cold for wintering over outdoors. Foliage will cascade somewhat over the edge of a large planter box.

CULINARY USE Flower bracts and foliage have a strong scent that is distinctive among the lavenders and inclines decidedly toward the menthol, eucalyptus, and balsamic range. Raw foliage tastes very astringent and petrol–like, and is generally too intense to be used culinarily in unaltered form, although a strong herb bread, weighted toward rosemary and sage seasoning, might benefit from the addition of a small amount of French lavender. The heavy flavor, reminiscent of both rosemary and camphor, precludes its use in desserts, most breads, and glazed flowers. However, grilling chicken with the foliage of this plant produces a unique flavor that, admittedly, one either loves or hates. Red meats and game are the best for limited experimentation with this formidable flavoring.

SPECIAL USES/COMMENTS Bloom is so frequent and lovely that it's hard to find a time when one can bear to shear back the plant for the sake of tidiness. Be resolute, however, and clip the foliage back firmly after winter or spring bloom to encourage a dense and sturdy canopy. The slightly antiseptic fragrance of *L. dentata* foliage creates a pleasant, clean smell in the home and around patients recuperating from illnesses. Treat as a fresh-cut flower or use the foliage to accent other cut garden flowers.

GREY FRENCH LAVENDER

COMMON NAME Grey (gray) French lavender (also sold as 'Candicans' or 'French Grey').

BOTANICAL NAME *Lavandula dentata* var. *candicans*.

FLOWER DESCRIPTION Very much like *L. dentata*, except smaller. Color of the corolla is duller and paler and the bracts less pronounced. The amount of bloom produced at any one time is noticeably less than that of the typical French lavender.

BLOOM PERIOD Sporadically from early to late summer.

PLANT AND FOLIAGE DESCRIPTION Grows up to 18 inches high and equally wide. Similar to the species form of French lavender except for its generally smaller size and noticeably grayer, more silvery foliage. Tomentose nature of this plant makes it white enough to show up among other plants on moonlit nights. Foliage is somewhat weaker and a bit more spindly than that of the common variety and will hold more moisture, so the plant is more likely to topple under the weight of rain or sprinkler irrigation.

HARDINESS AND PLANTING RANGE More tender than species French lavender. Thrives only in Zones 9 through 11 or down to about 20° F.

TYPICAL LANDSCAPE USE Because the amount and quality of bloom are so much less than for the species French lavender, this plant is usually treated as a foliage plant. Makes an excellent foil for dark-colored leaves of nearby plants. A skirt of low-growing, dark-foliaged ground cover such as thyme (*Thymus vulgaris*), bearberry (*Arctostaphylos uvaursi*), baby's tears (*Soleirolia soleirolli*), or *Scaevola* 'Mauve Clusters' will call attention to the silvery gray foliage. Because it's not as vigorous as the species form, grey French lavender is best used as an occasional accent or a focal-point plant.

This variety can be grown well in containers, which is fortunate since the plant will have to be brought indoors in many climates. Its small size makes it appropriate for more manageable pottery (under 16 inches in diameter), and it cascades a bit over the edge of a planter box.

CULINARY USE Generally the same as the species form, but the foliage is less pungent.

SPECIAL USES/COMMENTS Because rain, dew, and sprinkler irrigation can cause the limbs to droop, prune heavily after bloom for a more compact character.

Spike Lavender

The oldest known mention of *Lavandula spica*, according to Baron Frederic Charles Jean de Gingins's *Natural History of the Lavenders*, was in a book published in 1499 in Venice, Italy, by J. de Dondis of Padua. De Gingins also reports this species of lavender as native to southern France (including Provence), southeastern Spain (south of the Balearic Islands), and perhaps even near Florence, although there it might have been cultivated by Italian gardeners and not found in a wild state. Other authorities maintain that it is indigenous to the southern Alps, Portugal, and the lower elevations of Spain, below 1,800 feet.

Old references to an herb called Nardus Indica, Nard, or Spikenard, brought to the Mediterranean and the Middle East via the Silk Road have been linked to lavender. Some say lavender was used as a less costly substitute for this desirable, expensive herb used to perfume baths and oil the hair and body. A look at the origins of the word *nardus* reveals that the Latin word *spica* may have followed this plant around for nearly a thousand years.

> *Nard*, see spikenard
> *spikenard* (spik´närd´) noun
> 1. An aromatic perennial herb (*Nardostachys jatamansi*) of the Himalayan Mountains and China, having rose-purple flowers. Also called nard. 2. An ointment of antiquity, probably prepared from this aromatic plant of India. (Middle English, from Anglo-Norman, from Medieval Latin *spica nardi*: Latin *spica*, spike, ear + Latin *nardi*, genitive of *nardus*, nard.) (*The American Heritage Dictionary*, 3rd Edition)

Spike lavender does not have any named cultivars; although a recent cultivar named 'Helen Batchelder' is sometimes listed as *L. spica* and may very well be a selection of *L. latifolia*.

COMMON NAME   Spike lavender (also sold as Spica lavender, Nardus Italica, lavender spike, lesser lavender, Dutch lavender, and Spikenard).

BOTANICAL NAME   *Lavandula latifolia*.

FLOWER DESCRIPTION   Profuse bloomer with tall flower stems, growing up to 24 inches above the foliage and, unlike those of English lavenders, branched like a candelabra with three or more arms. Flower buds are packed into tight whorls spaced over a fairly long portion of the stem, and main flower head (not the more diminutive heads on the lower arms of the candelabra) is much narrower, longer, and more evenly tapered than those of most other lavenders, especially the round-headed English species and cultivars. This is not the most dramatically colored lavender flower—the corollas are a pale to medium violet and about ⅜ inch long, with the calyx a darker purple. Some people consider the unopened buds to be brilliant or showy.

BLOOM PERIOD A late-flowering species that blooms from June to late July or mid-August in Zone 7, noticeably later in California—with some flower stems into winter.

PLANT AND FOLIAGE DESCRIPTION Foliage fairly similar in size and color to that of *L. angustifolia*, although the leaves, which grow 1 to 1½ inches long and at least ¼ inch wide, are generally broader. Distinctive grayish blue-green leaves are awl-shaped and coarse, with blunt tips. Usually has more tomentose leaves than English lavenders, and bracts have one central rib, unlike the multiveined bracts of the English species.

HARDINESS AND PLANTING RANGE Although one catalog lists hardiness to -20° F, spike lavender has been known to succumb to temperatures in the 0° to -10° F range. Botanist Baron de Gingins confidently stated in 1826 that "*Lavande Spica* is always to be found in the region where olive trees grow." Perhaps a better way of phrasing this is if olives thrive in your yard or area, then many types of lavender, including *L. latifolia*, will prosper.

TYPICAL LANDSCAPE USE As a single accent plant or in large masses for a drift of colorful foliage. Mixes well with dark green foliage. Narrow flower heads on the tall stems make for a very nice vertical element in a landscape design. If the flower heads are left to rot off the stems, the stems make a great place for garden spiders to spin their webs.

CULINARY USE Resinous overtones are not as pronounced as those of *L. dentata*, but this is not the ideal lavender for desserts and bread. Burning the foliage while grilling meats helps to tame the plant's wild flavor.

SPECIAL USES/COMMENTS Tolerates soils with a lower pH (more acidic) than English lavenders.

Spike lavender may have been the most popular medicinal lavender among herbalists of earlier times. Its pungent, astringent aroma and flavor are said to indicate its medicinal value, including its proven antibacterial benefit. In 1991 spike lavender oil accounted for about 20 percent (71 tons) of the world production of lavender oils.

Lavandin

Technically, lavandin is a natural interspecific hybrid of English lavender (*L. angustifolia*) and spike lavender (*L. latifolia*). The plants resulting from this cross usually produce only sterile seed, and all new lavandin plants are obtained from cuttings. The first natural lavandin hybrid was found in 1828.

The lavandin cultivar 'Abrialii' (also known as 'Abrial' and 'Abrialis') was originally found prior to 1935 and was the mainstay of the French lavender-oil industry until the 1970s. Over time, the 'Abrialii' cultivar became ravaged by mycoplasm, a so-called wasting ailment that caused the plants to yellow and rapidly die. Mycoplasm refers to any of the numerous parasitic, pathogenic microorganisms of the genus *Mycoplasma*. As a result, the fields of French 'Abrialii' lavandin were rendered viable for only three or four years as opposed to the normal eight to ten years.

The lavandin cultivar 'Grosso' was discovered about 1972 as a result of attempts to replace 'Abrialii' and has been the dominant cultivar since 1975. Another variety, named 'Super', was discovered in the foothills of the Alps (Provençal Pre-Alps) in 1956. Currently, about three-fourths of the French lavandin oil crop is from 'Grosso' and the rest is divided between 'Abrialii', 'Super', and a cultivar similar to 'Abrialii' called 'Sumain'.

Harvesting of true wild lavender grown from self-sown seed represented 90 percent of the French harvest—a mere 1 or 2 tons of oil—in the early 1920s. By the 1990s, cultivation of lavandin in France had risen to 28,000 acres, yielding 936 to 1,102 tons of lavandin oil. Much of the oil crop is used to scent laundry detergents and soaps.

A perfume chemist would describe lavandin oils in general as fruity, fatty, harsh, turpentinelike, eucalyptus fresh, camphoraceous, herbaceous, sweet, aromatic, and possessing a warm wood smell. Even without considering the nuances of their oil quality and their increased oil production, lavandin cultivars make beautiful landscape plants.

All lavandins are much less susceptible to fungal attacks than the English lavenders.

In the United States, the oil of lavandin 'Grosso' is becoming popular as the superior lavender aroma for soaps, room fresheners, and scented candles and culinary uses. It is more pungent or astringent than another popular lavandin called 'Provence'. The essential oil of 'Grosso' has been described as having a harsh, terpenic note.

COMMON NAME   Lavender 'Grosso' (also sold as lavandin 'Grosso', 'Fat Spike lavender').

BOTANICAL NAME   *Lavandula* x *intermedia* 'Grosso' (L. *angustifolia* 'Grosso').

FLOWER DESCRIPTION   Rotund, long flower heads of 'Grosso' are showy and 3 to 6 inches long and nearly 1 inch wide (hence, another name for this variety, 'Fat Spike'). Flower head is set on a stem up to 2 feet long. Young flower buds, before they open, are a mixture of green suffused with violet. Open corollas are a rich violet with some dark purple—only the blossoms of *L. pinnata*, *L. multifida*, and *L. canariensis* are a richer purple-violet. All three are members of the Pterostachys—the winged spikes—grouping of lavenders.

BLOOM PERIOD   Mid-June to mid-July in the eastern United States in Zone 7. In northern California (Zone 9), profusely in July; if pruned back firmly in midsummer, a smaller display appears in late summer or early fall. Bloom time similar from Zone 9 down to Zone 7 (or warmest portions of Zone 6), but plant may not have a second flowering.

PLANT AND FOLIAGE DESCRIPTION   One of the most delightful foliage colors of all the lavenders, a strong, true gray-green, with a decidedly bluish undertone and without the more tomentose features of some forms of *L. dentata*. Thick, medium-width leaves are long and tapered and form a dense, well-behaved canopy that is quite attractive, even when the plant is not in bloom. 'Grosso' remains truly evergreen within its preferred zone.

Unlike all other lavenders, this plant naturally grows much wider than its height—on average 8 to 16 inches tall and up to 3 feet wide. Flower stems are very inclined to curve gently outward from the plant, and a single specimen grown apart from other plants may have many curved flower stems lying gracefully on the ground, with the flower heads less than a foot above the soil. Where 'Grosso' is packed in with other plants, the flower heads elegantly wave in the breeze up to 2 feet above the ground.

HARDINESS AND PLANTING RANGE   This plant, hardy to 0° F and somewhat lower, is lumped into the vague category "hardy," but is not as cold resistant as *L. angustifolia*. At the low end of its range, 'Grosso' is unable to withstand continuous cold without snow cover or some protective covering, but results may be mixed. Some catalogs say all lavandins will grow in Zone 5, -10° to -20° F, while others rate these plants at -20° F. A safer approach would start with the best spots in Zone 6, -10° to 0° F.

TYPICAL LANDSCAPE USE   A glorious plant in mass plantings; if it is set closely together in parallel rows (about 36 inches apart), the curved flower stems bunch up and stand taller, and the stems from opposing rows meet to form a noticeably darker, more richly colored violet band where they mingle midrow. If the planting is tight enough in both directions, a marvelous crosshatching of shimmering dark purple-violet coloration becomes visible between the rows.

Individual plants make good showy specimens in the landscape, but plenty of room should be left around the plant for the flower stems to display their natural, sumptuous curves. Use a mulch to keep dirt from being splattered on foliage and flowers. In humid climates, a mulch of white sand (not salty beach sand), 1 to 2 inches deep, may be very helpful for the health of the plant and cause the essential oil content to rise by 28 to 771 percent.

CULINARY USE   To the nose, this is one of the more robust varieties of lavandin. The aroma of the foliage, calyxes, and corollas is more suggestive of camphor, terpenes, and eucalyptus than that of English lavender, but is not as intense as that of *L. dentata*. The stronger, heartier flavor precludes use in most dessert and bread recipes. 'Grosso' foliage and flowers are good to experiment with when grilling, making hearty meat-based soups and stews, or concocting marinades for red meats.

SPECIAL USES/COMMENTS   This hybrid produces only sterile seed and therefore must be propagated from cuttings. 'Grosso' will not produce seedlings in garden mulch, so you will need to purchase named variety plants or propagate them from cuttings.

COMMON NAME   Lavender 'Provence' (also sold as lavandin 'Provence', French lavender).

BOTANICAL NAME   *Lavandula* x *intermedia* 'Provence'.

FLOWER DESCRIPTION   Large flower heads, often 3 inches tall and ⅞ inch wide. As with many lavenders, a few individual flowers may be scattered along stem below actual flower head. Blooms are not as richly colored as a 'Grosso' flower, but are a solid violet with light purple highlights. Because of its straight flower stem and prolific bloom, the slightly paler color of 'Provence' is counterbalanced by its abundant display.

Flower aroma is both powerful and sweet, sometimes also described as heady, grassy, fruity, herbaceous, and mildly woody. This plant lacks much of the camphor/eucalyptuslike overtones that make other lavandins more intense and spicy. It is gaining popularity for its potential in perfumes, potpourris, sachets, lavender wands, and culinary uses.

BLOOM PERIOD   Mid-June to mid-July in the eastern United States in Zone 7. In more moderate zones, from early to late July, about two to four weeks after *L. angustifolia*.

PLANT AND FOLIAGE DESCRIPTION   Leaves typically longer, wider, and grayer than the species form of English lavender. Foliage gray-green but less gray than 'Grosso' and grows to 12 to 18 inches tall and slightly wider. Flower stems often tower 12 to 16 inches above the foliage, which looks better with a tight clipping each year after bloom. Canopy can be cut back to create cute little "buttons" 8 to 10 inches high and 1 foot wide; new growth will quickly fill in to cover the stubble and pale yellow leaves exposed by shearing.

HARDINESS AND PLANTING RANGE   Similar climate range to 'Grosso'. Hardy to 0° F and perhaps lower.

TYPICAL LANDSCAPE USE   As an accent plant, in mass plantings, and in pottery at least 24 inches in diameter. Plant every 18 inches for a reasonably quick fill-in of foliage. If planted every 24 inches and given a yearly trim, foliage of adjacent plants may just touch. Also has potential as a formally trained topiary, neat hedge, or naturally irregular hedge.

CULINARY USE   Perhaps the sweetest of the lavandins and therefore appropriate for desserts, ice creams, sorbets, and breads, as well as for heartier fare. Because 'Provence' is culinarily stronger in all respects than English lavender, you may not want to use as much as is called for in recipes using the English variety. Heat and cooking tempers the intensity of lavender/lavandin aromas, and you may need to experiment for appropriate seasoning to taste.

SPECIAL USES/COMMENTS Because 'Provence', being a lavandin, produces more oil than English lavenders and is so highly valued for its sweet aroma, this would be the first variety to experiment with in distilling and making tinctures in limited amounts. You'll need to harvest about 4 pounds of blossoms to make 1 ounce of oil, or 66½ pounds of flowers to distill about 17 ounces. With English lavender, around 8 to 16 pounds of flowers are needed for each ounce of oil.

Other lavandin hybrids to watch for in mail-order catalogs and local nurseries are 'Abrialii' ('Abrial', 'Abrialis'), 'Alba', 'Dutch', 'Fred Boutin', 'Grappenhall', 'Grey Hedge', 'Old English', 'Seal', 'Silver Gray', 'Standard', and 'Super'.

"lavender, sweet lavender;
come and buy my lavender,
hide it in your trousseau, lady fair.
let its lovely fragrance flow
over you from head to toe,
lightening on your eyes, your cheek, your hair."

CUMBERLAND CLARK • *Flower Song Book* 1929

Pterostachys Lavenders — Winged Spikes

Unlike the preceding groupings, where the lavenders were reviewed together by species, *Pterostachys* is a broad category of lavenders of many species. The name comes from the Greek word *pteron*, meaning "feather or wing"—thus the name *pterodactyl* for flying reptiles from the Jurassic period. In this case, *Pterostachys* is a reference to the flowers growing like winged spikes on the flower head. Some of the plants in this category have no fragrance, one smells bad, and others smell somewhat like a "true" lavender. No essential oils are extracted from any of these plants, and this group happens to include many of the most frost-tender varieties. Among the species lavender that fit into this category are the following, which are treated briefly one by one.

COMMON NAMES	BOTANICAL NAMES
'Goodwin Creek Grey'	*L.* x *dentata*
'Sweet Lavender' ('Silver Sweet Lavender')	*L. heterophylla* (*L. dentata* x *L. latifolia*)
'Fernleaf' ('Pubescens', 'Lavender Lace')	*L. multifida* (*L. pubescens*)
'Canary Island'	*L. canariensis* (*L. multifida* var. *canariensis*, *L. pinnata* var. 'Buchii')
'Jagged Lavender' ('Pinnata Lavender')	*L. pinnata* (*L.* 'Buchii', *L. pinnata* var. 'Buchii')

COMMON NAME 'Goodwin Creek Grey'.

BOTANICAL NAME *Lavendula* x. *dentata*.

    This may be a hybrid of *L. dentata* x *L. lanata*. It can't be crossed with *L. hetero-phylla*, as some catalogs suggest, because it is already a cross and therefore sterile.

FLOWER DESCRIPTION Small corollas are dark purple with tall stems and narrow, long, and tapered flower heads. Flower heads do not stand out as much as those of other lavenders, such as French or Spanish, and the plant is often treated as a foliage plant.

BLOOM PERIOD Midsummer.

PLANT AND FOLIAGE DESCRIPTION Discovered in 1991 by growers at Goodwin Creek Gardens in Williams, Oregon. Its special feature is its glorious foliage, which is a clean, smooth silver-gray. This unique lavender is gaining rapid favor among passionate "lavenderists" for the ornamental value of its attractive and slightly tomentose foliage. Leaves have indented margins like those of French lavender. Plant grows to 2 feet tall and wide. (For the record, the most silver-leaved lavender is reputedly the *L. angustifolia* 'Silver Frost'.)

HARDINESS AND PLANTING RANGE Listed as a "tender" variety by some catalogs, but is rated by Goodwin Creek Gardens to grow in Zones 6 (-10° to 0° F) through 11.

TYPICAL LANDSCAPE USE Good lavender to present as an accent or highlight—one properly placed specimen will really make an impact. Try planting it against a dark-colored boulder to set off the silver-gray foliage. A skirt of round gray river or ocean rocks will also provide a very nice complement to the foliage color.

CULINARY USE Not well known yet. Since it probably originated from *L. dentata*, flowers and foliage are more camphoraceous and piny than English lavenders, making it, in all probability, a plant for more cautious, prudent culinary experiments.

SPECIAL USES/COMMENTS Try planting in a special terra-cotta pot, half-wine barrel, or planter box to place as a garden or patio accent.

COMMON NAME 'Sweet Lavender' (also sold as 'Silver Sweet Lavender').

BOTANICAL NAME *Lavendula heterophylla* (*L. dentata* x *L. latifolia*).

FLOWER DESCRIPTION Long, narrow flower heads have pale blue-violet flowers on tall straight stems. Although flowers have a very slight undertone of camphor, they are rated as the sweetest scented lavender outside of the English types.

BLOOM PERIOD Late summer.

PLANT AND FOLIAGE DESCRIPTION A fast-growing plant that can reach 3 feet tall and equally wide. Gray-green, felted foliage with long narrow leaves that are sometimes serrated. Some of the older leaves near the base of the plant are partially or totally dentate (toothed). Gets sooty mold easily; use drip irrigation wherever possible to help avoid this disease.

HARDINESS AND PLANTING RANGE To 15° F.

TYPICAL LANDSCAPE USE Good plant for large pottery, tubs, and planter boxes. Can be massed in the landscape for a wash of foliage color.

CULINARY USE With experimentation, this plant may be used much like English lavender and its cultivars, in all recipes from desserts to meat dishes.

SPECIAL USES/COMMENTS Makes an excellent tub or potted plant.

"lavender, sweet-briar, orris. here
shall beauty make her pomander,
her sweet-balls for to lay in clothes
that wrap her as the leaves the rose."

KATHERINE TYNAN   •   *The Choice*

COMMON NAME 'Fernleaf' (also sold as 'Pubescens', 'Lavender Lace').

BOTANICAL NAME *Lavendula multifida* (*L. pubescens*).

In the late 1500s, the Flemish botanist-physician Carolus Clusius (Charles de Lecluse) found a rare lavender in the hills of Spain near Málaga and gave it the name of *L. multifido folio*; we know it today as *L. multifida*. It is also indigenous to Portugal.

FLOWER DESCRIPTION Corollas ½ inch long are a royal deep violet, one of the richest violets to be found among all lavenders. Corollas arranged in a tight circle, like a violet skirt, around the flower head, and flower spike often has three shoots per stalk, like Neptune's trident. These singular or triple-headed flower stalks are very decorative, 6 to 20 inches tall, and usually rather long and sinuous. Alas, 'Fernleaf' has no scent.

BLOOM PERIOD Some almost all spring and summer in the mildest climates or indoors.

PLANT AND FOLIAGE DESCRIPTION Finely cut foliage is soft, gray, and tomentose, growing to 2 feet tall and equally wide. Leaves are bipinnate, having a fernlike leaf pattern also somewhat resembling that of a small locust-tree leaf or cut-leaf chrysanthemum, soft, and hairy. Foliage has a strong smell that is not at all like the classic lavender smell—some people state categorically that it stinks; others merely call it pungent.

HARDINESS AND PLANTING RANGE Very tender and hardy only in Zones 9 (30° to 40° F) through 11.

TYPICAL LANDSCAPE USE This is an excellent container plant. In most climates, it must be grown in a pot that can be moved each winter to a sheltered place.

CULINARY USE None.

SPECIAL USES/COMMENTS Can be treated as an annual bedding plant, but in this case will produce only foliage.

COMMON NAME 'Canary Island'.

BOTANICAL NAME *Lavendula. canariensis* (*L. multifida* var. *canariensis*, *L. multifida* ssp. *canariensis*, *L. pinnata* var. 'Buchii').

FLOWER DESCRIPTION Flower heads are longer than those of 'Fernleaf' lavender, but are otherwise similar.

BLOOM PERIOD In a mild climate, nearly all year.

PLANT AND FOLIAGE DESCRIPTION Fernlike leaves are very similar to those of *L. multifida*, but are larger and of a glossy, smooth, robust bright green color. Grows to 3 feet tall and 3 feet wide.

HARDINESS AND PLANTING RANGE Somewhat hardier than 'Fernleaf' lavender.

TYPICAL LANDSCAPE USE Because this shrub is so easily killed by light frosts, plant it in an attractive planter box or terra-cotta pot that can be moved indoors.

CULINARY USE Coarse scent emulates turpentine; it has no culinary uses.

SPECIAL USES/COMMENTS Works as an annual bedding plant when an attractive display of foliage is desired.

COMMON NAME 'Jagged Lavender' (also sold as 'Pinnata Lavender').

This is an awkward common name for a plant that looks so much like *L. multifida*, or 'Fernleaf', that the two are often confused with and sold as each other. In the late 1700s, Carolus Linnaeus, the famous pioneering Swedish botanist, classified a plant collected on Madeira Island, near the Canary Islands, as *L. pinée*, now called *L. pinnata*.

BOTANICAL NAME *L. pinnata* (*L.* 'Buchii', *L. pinnata* var. 'Buchii').

FLOWER DESCRIPTION Long corollas, ¼ to ⅜ inch, are a deep lavender and, like those of 'Fernleaf', are arranged in a tight circle resembling a violet skirt (winged spike) around the flower head. Flower spike also has three shoots per stalk, like Neptune's trident. These singular or triple-headed flower stalks are 8 to 14 inches tall, making 'Jagged Lavender' a very decorative plant.

BLOOM PERIOD Frequently for a long period of time in mild areas or indoors.

PLANT AND FOLIAGE DESCRIPTION Like 'Fernleaf', this plant also has finely cut, lacy bipinnate foliage that is soft, gray, and tomentose.

HARDINESS AND PLANTING RANGE Best reserved for the warmest parts of Zone 9 and in Zones 10 and 11.

TYPICAL LANDSCAPE USE Excellent container plant, especially in those climates where it must be moved to a frost-free place in winter.

CULINARY USE None.

SPECIAL USES/COMMENTS Some gardeners like the foliage enough to treat this lavender like an annual plant in cold-winter climates.

"best among all good plants for hot, sandy soils
are the ever blessed lavender and rosemary,
delicious old garden bushes that one can hardly dissociate."

MISS JEKYLL • *Home and Garden* 1900

planting
and
cultivating
Lavenders

Lavenders love to bask in the sun, and the longer the sun shines on your lavender patch, the more your plants will flourish and bloom. Considering their Mediterranean origins, these shrubs need, at very least, four hours of direct sunlight per day. Although most lavenders will grow in up to 50 percent filtered sunlight, such plants will produce little bloom, and their foliage will tend to look weedy and disheveled if not sheared back periodically.

Once you decide on a sunny planting site, take a look at—and a feel of—the soil. To grow and flourish, lavenders need excellent drainage. Nothing kills otherwise hardy *Lavandula* faster than poor drainage or heavy, soggy clay soils. Lavender will tolerate clayey loam (silty) soils better than many other drought-resistant plants, but when planted in too much clay—or if watered too heavily near the crown (top) of the root system—it will succumb to root rot, the major disease of the genus. Root rot is a condition that can take hold of nearly any plant, causing all the leaves on the plant, or on individual branches, to go limp at once and then turn yellow. Since lavender leaves are so stiff and diminutive, they don't really go limp, but turn yellow and then brown. Once these symptoms are visible, it's too late to save the plant. Any extra watering at this point not only has no benefit but may actually speed up the plant's demise.

SOIL AND FERTILIZER

When it comes to the need for fertilizer, lavenders are amazingly self-reliant. They prefer a soil containing lime (called chalk in England) and with a pH (measure of acidity or alkalinity) in the range of 6.4 to 8.3. A soil with a 7.0 pH is neutral (neither acid nor alkaline); one with 6.4 (common in the average garden) is barely acid (the pH of lemon juice is 1.3 to 2.4); and one with an alkalinity of 8.3 is somewhat closer to the alkali soils found in a desert (pH 9 to 11). In a soil where the pH is not too far off from the ideal (less than 1.5 points on either side of 7.0), lavenders need little in the way of extra nutrients.

You may wish to take a sample of your soil to a local plant nursery or soil amendment retailer and have a lab analysis done for pH and for the major nutrients (nitrogen, phosphorus, potash, and calcium), as well as for organic matter content. Ask the nursery or store staff to analyze the results and make recommendations for the proper amendments.

If the pH of your soil is too acidic, add 3 to 8 pounds (based on soil composition: 3 pounds for sandy soils, up to 8 pounds for heavy clay) of ground limestone or oyster-shell flour per 100 square feet of planting area. When the soil pH is above 8.3, use ½ pound of powdered (agricultural) sulfur per 100 square feet in sandy soil or 2 pounds in all other soil types.

Giving lavender too much fertilizer is a waste of time and materials and may actually cause problems. In one study, fertilizer given to lavenders had no effect on increasing their essential oil content or aroma. Although overfertilization may result in a more lush growth, this same growth is more tender to early frosts. Too much fertilizer may also make the foliage more vulnerable to fungal attack. In most soils, you need to fertilize only if there is poor growth or slightly pale or yellow foliage (not followed by browning, which is a sign of root rot), indicating a nutrient deficiency in the soil.

Commercial growers in France use less than .10 a pound per 100 square feet of ammonium sulfate (21 percent nitrogen), superphosphate (20 percent phosphorous), and potassium sulfate (54 percent potassium). (The sulfur compounds in the ammonium sulfate and the potassium sulfate help adjust the alkalinity of the soil, due to the presence of limestone, down to the slightly alkaline pH that lavender plants prefer.)

Some growers in the summer-rain areas of the United States apply a judicious amount of 15-15-15 fertilizer (containing 15 percent of each of the major elements—nitrogen, phosphorus, and potash) every three or four weeks, especially the first year after planting. Alternatively, an organic granular fertilizer, well-composted manure, or worm castings can be used. You should stop all fertilizing at least three weeks before the first expected frost in your area. Some gardeners apply a mixture of powdered chicken manure and lime ¼ inch deep around the plant in the fall only—spring and summer application may burn the foliage.

TIPS FOR PLANTING

Even when working with good soil, it's important to plant your *Lavandula* on a well-drained raised mound. The soil amendments in a lavender mound don't have to be organic in the sense of fibrous, just fast draining. Here's the best way to give lavender a good start in your garden.

- Use a spading fork to loosen the native soil where you want to plant. Insert the fork into the ground and rock back on the handle to heave and fracture the soil.

- Mix about one part native soil with one part, or less, *very* well-rotted straw mixed with manure (turkey, chicken, or horse bedding) and one or two parts of *round* river rock, in mixed sizes up to ½ to ¾ inch in diameter. Don't use crushed rock with angular facets, which will compact over time. Avoid adding too many high-fiber soil amendments, as they may actually encourage root rot by holding water. Since fertilizers are unnecessary for lavender planted in most soils, you may wish simply to buy a sandy-loam topsoil and add some river rock when building your mound. The amount of amendments should gradually diminish as the planting hole meets the native soil so the roots can adjust to the soil in which they will eventually grow.

- Make the mound 8 to 18 inches tall and 16 to 24 inches wide for each 1 gallon-size (or smaller) plant. The whole construction should be at least 4 to 9 inches tall after it has settled (amended soil can settle by 50 percent). The more rain in your area, the higher you'll need to make the mound for adequate drainage.

- Dig out a shallow planting spot in the mound. Form a cone of rocky soil in the bottom of the hole, spread the roots of the lavender over the cone, and cover them with the gravel-soil mix.

- Water thoroughly.

- In true, nonhumid Mediterranean climates, you can cover the ground to within 6 inches of the stem with any attractive mulch. In humid areas, a beige, light gray, or white mulch made of sand (not salty beach sand) or attractive pebbles will help reflect light and heat to prevent fungal problems. Research suggests that a sand mulch actually decreases the occurrence of frost heaving, when the melting and freezing of the ground tear the roots as the plant is pushed up toward the soil surface.

- If you plan to use drip irrigation, place a ½-gallon-per-hour emitter 12 to 18 inches from the stem of each plant or at the base of the planting mound. Once the emitters are running, a narrow wet spot forms on the soil surface, becoming much wider just below the surface where the roots grow. If soil preparation, watering, and mulching are done correctly, the water from the emitters, spreading slowly sideways below the ground, will keep the new lavender roots moistened. Placing the emitters at the base of the mound prevents irrigation water from rotting the roots.

This is a novel and inexpensive way to build attractive planting mounds for large areas of your yard—almost any size if you have enough wood chips. The technique is especially helpful in places where the soil is clayey or there is a high water table or standing water at times. The mound-planting technique can help those in otherwise marginal situations make lavender flourish. In good climates and situations, lavender will be even healthier. I have used this technique only in a moderate-summer climate with a moderating marine influence. A very similar approach is popular in German gardens and elsewhere around the world. You may have to make some changes in your area and experiment with your soil and climate.

- Stockpile chunky wood chips (not sawdust, which doesn't drain) from local tree-trimming services. They save money by dumping a load of chips at your garden.
- Build an active compost pile from the tree chips—the greener the better. Because tree chips are so high in carbon, layer or mix them with some manure, about one part manure to three or four parts chips. Pile this mixture of high-carbon and high-nitrogen materials up to 100 percent higher than you'll want the final mound. Water each layer as you go to make sure all materials are moist.
- Cover the mound with a soil cap at least 4 inches thick—the thicker, the better. Use a mixture of 50 percent very well-rotted straw with animal manure or other compost and 50 percent native soil for the top layer. The soil cap ensures neutral soil temperature, balanced nutrition, and good initial growth for the transplants. Because of the soil cap, you can plant the day the mound is covered with the soil mixture.
- Plant into the soil cap and water thoroughly. To determine the spacing, place each plant 50 percent of their mature width apart. In other words, if the variety of English lavender you're planting grows to 18 inches wide, place the plants 9 inches apart in all directions.
- Use 10 sheets of overlapping newspapers to cover all exposed soil, and cover with a weed-free mulch to cover the soil cap and suppress all weed seedlings (like a "biodegradable herbicide").
- Within one year or more, the mounds will settle down and the lavender will root into the native soil.

The best watering schemes are based on information, not intuition or guessing. Your lavender plants can flourish if not watered too heavily or too sparingly. If it rains where you live, summer showers may provide all the moisture your lavender requires or even may provide too much. But in dry Mediterranean areas, some judicious summer irrigation will improve foliage growth and produce more blooming stems. The standard for determining the amount of irrigation your lavender needs is the amount of watering recommended for lawns by a local newspaper or the county Cooperative Extension (look under the county government pages in your telephone book). A recommendation of 1 inch of water per week during July translates to 60 gallons of water spread over 100 square feet.

To determine what your sprinkler puts out, place four to six straight-sided buckets in four to six places under the spray pattern. Run the sprinkler until there is an average depth of 1 inch of water in the buckets—an amount equal to 60 gallons for every 100 square feet of the sprinkler's pattern.

With drip irrigation, count the number of emitters per 100 square feet. (The number of emitters is originally determined by the soil type. A sandy soil would have emitters very close together compared with a heavy clay soil, because sand drains quickly and clay spreads water to the sides more. The goal is to have the moist spots in the soil below each emitter merge together within an hour or so. This is figured out by testing some emitters at various spacings and time intervals.) If each emitter puts out ½ gallon per hour, divide the number of emitters in half to arrive at gallons per hour. If, for example, your system has 28 emitters, it is putting out 14 gallons per hour. Then divide 60 gallons of water by 14 gallons per hour to get the number of hours that the system needs to run to equal 1 inch of water or 60 gallons per 100 square feet. In this example, 60 divided by 14 equals 4.3 hours.

Lavender, however, requires much less water than a lawn to thrive and bloom abundantly. In a mild coastal California climate, lavenders need only 10 to 30 percent of the water a lawn requires, that is, only 6 to 18 gallons each week for every 100 square feet of planting. Applying the above example for drip irrigation, the 4.3 hours needed to deliver 60 gallons of water per 100 square feet is multiplied by .1 to .3 to equal .4 to .13 hours. In hot, dry desert conditions, lavenders need 40 to 60 percent of the water recommended for a lawn—24 to 36 gallons per week.

It's best to water with a drip-irrigation system so the moisture is applied even with, or beyond, the dripline (outer perimeter) of the foliage. Watering *between* plants, instead of under their foliage, helps prevent deadly root rot. If you must use a sprinkler, make sure the plants are in very well-drained soil. Be sure to irrigate early in the morning so the morning sunlight can dry the foliage. Avoid watering on overcast days if possible. If you have just a few plants and want to hand water, be sure to keep the hose or sprinkling can away from the base of the shrub and water outside the edge of the foliage. Remember, the roots extend well beyond the dripline of each plant.

DISEASES, PESTS, AND WEED CONTROL

The three big diseases of lavender are root rot, mildew, and rust. Root rot, due to any number of species of *Phytothphora*, is best taken care of with proper planting techniques. If an occasional plant, or any portion thereof, suddenly yellows and then turns brown, it probably has root rot. Pull the entire plant and take it to the Cooperative Extension, a Master Gardener's group, or a good nursery for an exact diagnosis of the cause. Then replant on a small mound with a well-drained soil.

There are many rusts and mildews that can affect lavenders foliage. Rusts usually cause patches of brown or rust-colored foliage. Mildews add a distinctive powdery whitish or grayish look to the foliage. Both are an indication of too much watering of the foliage, summer rains, or high humidity. You can't control the rain or humidity, but try switching to drip irrigation if you're presently using sprinklers. Fungus can start on the dead leaves and then move on to living tissue. Cy Hyde, of Well-Sweep Herb Farm in Port Murray, New Jersey, says you can keep fungi from getting a foothold (leafhold) by spreading your fingers open and, on a dry day, running them from the ground up through the foliage to break off all dead foliage. Rake and collect the fallen dead material and compost or burn.

If you've planted your lavenders properly and you water appropriately and only as needed, you've circumvented root rot, the major disease. As for other pests and diseases, the Western hemisphere thus far has apparently been spared the fatal shab disease that has maimed

English and other European lavender crops from time to time. It's important, however, to be aware of shab disease symptoms, which are very similar to those of root rot. After May, young lavender shoots afflicted with shab turn yellow and wilt, and branches may subsequently die. If this happens, immediately take specimens of the damaged foliage to your local Cooperative Extension, Master Gardener's group, or nursery for proper identification. When in doubt, burn the affected plants or toss them in the garbage.

One mainly visual nuisance that affects the blooms and foliage of lavender plants in spring and early summer is an annual proliferation of spittlebugs, known outside the United States as foam cicads. The immature nymphs of this insect secrete a bubbly mass that surrounds their soft bodies for protection and clings to plant stems as frothy white blobs of "spittle." These insects, which otherwise do little harm to plants, are easy to disperse with a firm spray from a hose nozzle or with a simple insecticidal-soap spray. This is often done just before photographing a blooming stand.

As with any plant, weeds should be pulled or mulched down, as they will rob moisture and nutrients from lavender—not to mention that a weed-free stand of lavender is a splendid sight. Another reason to keep large weeds away from lavender plants is that weed foliage may increase air humidity around the lavender, thus increasing the chances of foliage mildew or rust.

Do not place organic mulches near the trunk of lavender plants. As mentioned earlier, a white sand (not salty beach sand) mulch in humid climates will greatly increase essential oil production and improve the plant's growth by reducing the risk of contracting various mildews and fungi. If you use artificial weed barriers near lavender, choose a type that breathes—meaning a woven landscape fabric, not plastic sheeting—so the soil itself can drain and breathe.

The British dependency of Gibraltar, the famous "Rock" located at the entrance to the Mediterranean Sea on the southernmost point of the Iberian Peninsula, is a natural home to *L. dentata* (French lavender) and *L. multifida* ('Fernleaf' lavender). To find out what plants actually make the best companions to lavender—not just in our romantic assumptions—we need only to look at a list of plants native to Gibraltar.

Some of the following plants thrive only in the mildest parts of Zones 9, 10, and 11. Others are practically unheard of in nurseries in the United States, but other species from the same genus may provide a similar look and feel the flora indigenous to Gibraltar. For example, the ornamental pistacio (*Pistacia chinensis*) is more common in Zones 9, 10, and 11 than the Mastic, lentisc tree (*Pistacia lentiscus*). Also, the coffeeberry tree (*Rhamnus californica*) is a native Californian plant, while the Mediterranean or Italian buckthorn (*Rhamnus alaternus*) is less well known.

Becoming familiar with this list is one of the best ways to begin constructing a garden that mimics the native habitat of lavender. Similar comparisons can be made with parts of Spain, France, Italy, and various Mediterranean islands.

TREES

Carob (*Ceratonia siliqua*)

Mastic, lentisc (*Pistacia lentiscus*)

Turpentine (*Pistacia terebinthus*)

Olive (*Olea europaea*)

Sweet bay, laurel (*Laurus nobilis*)

SHRUBS

Gray-leaved cistus (*Cistus albidus*)

Mediterranean or Italian buckthorn
  (*Rhamnus alaternus*)

Rosemary (*Rosmarinus officinalis*)

Sage-leaved cistus (*Cistus salviifolius*)

Narrow-leaved fringed rue (*Ruta
  angustifolia*)

BULBS

Common gladiolus (*Gladiolus communes*)

Great round-headed leek (*Allium ampeloprasum*)

VINES

Honeysuckle (*Lonicera implexa*)

Virgin's bower (*Clematis cirrhosa*)

A list from Provence, the famous lavender district in France, includes the following companion trees, shrubs, and perennials. Again, you may have to substitute a different species more adapted to your climate.

TREES

Acacia (*Acacia* sp.)

Atlas cedar (*Cedrus atlantica*)

Beech (*Fagus* sp.)

Birch (*Betula* sp.)

Cedar of Lebanon (*Cedrus libani*)

Chestnut (*Castenea* sp.)

Cork oak (*Quercus suber*)

Cypress (*Cupressus* sp.)

London plane (*Platanus acerfolia*)

Maple (*Acer* sp.)

Mastic, lentisc (*Pistachia lentiscus*)

Persimmon (*Diospyros kaki*)

Pine, Aleppo (*Pinus halepensis*)

Pines (*Pinus* sp.)

Poplar (*Populus* sp.)

Spruce (*Picea* sp.)

Walnut (*Juglans* sp.)

SHRUBS

Hazel (*Corylus* sp.)

Spurge (*Euphorbia* sp.)

Strawberry tree (*Arburus unedo*)

PERENNIALS

Anemone (*Anemone* sp.)

Clary sage (*Salvia sclarea*)

Crane's bill (*Geranium* sp.)

Iris (*Iris* sp.)

Globe thistle, artichoke (*Cynara scolymus*)

Mint (*Mentha* sp.)

Peony (*Paeonia* sp.)

Tarragon (*Artemesia dracunculus*)

If your garden space is limited, or you want a Mediterranean look for a sunny terrace or patio, you may want to plant lavenders in containers. For this type of cultivation, choose large receptacles made of a "breathing" material like terra-cotta, and use a light, well-drained potting mixture without fungal spores. Purchased potting mixes are sterile to begin with. Choose a mix that derives at least some of its drainage from inert nonorganic elements such as sand (not salty beach sand), small volcanic rock, vermiculite, and perlite. Organic drainage amendments like sphagnum moss, compost, and peat moss hold on to water and can cause root rot, so avoid potting mixes that contain too much organic fiber.

Since the best potting soils for lavenders drain so well, they will soon become low in nutrition due to the leaching out of nutrients when plants are watered. Container-grown lavender requires regular fertilization with any of the slow-release fertilizer pellets or granules available at local nurseries. Examples include 14-14-14 (14 percent nitrogen, phosphorus, and potash), 15-15-15, and 20-20-20. Apply several or more times each year according the directions on the label.

Indoor gardening is certainly more work than outdoor growing, and requires special hardware; it is, however, the only way many species of lavender can survive in cold-winter areas. Or, if you live where summer humidity is high and have a dehumidifier in your house, your lavender might just prefer to be indoors (even if it's cooler than the ideal temperature for lavender) because the foliage won't suffer so much fungus and rot from excess humidity.

To begin indoor gardening, plant your *Lavandula* collection in a fast-draining, nonhumus potting soil. (Hydroponic planting, a system of growing plants with their roots in a solution of nutrient-rich water, is obviously out of the question for lavender.) The best place for indoor lavender culture is a sunny south-facing window, bay window, or enclosed porch, but since this plant originated in the Mediterranean basin and loves long hours of light, additional artificial light is necessary, even in the brightest indoor settings.

Fluorescent tubes are three times more efficient in converting electrical energy to light (and last 10 times longer) than typical incandescent bulbs, provide the best artificial-light sources available for growing plants in the home. These tubes are sold in many sizes and shapes, although the straight 2-, 4- or 8-foot lengths are the most popular with growers. Special fluorescent tubes for growing indoors have a higher output in the red range to balance the blue output of typical fluorescent bulbs and are sold as Gro-lamps. Many indoor gardeners use the two kinds of bulbs in combination, one Gro-lamp to each one or two of the cool white tubes.

The typical fluorescent light fixtures make it practically impossible to produce too much light for lavender; this sun-loving plant will flourish under special high-intensity lamps containing three or four fluorescent tubes and putting out about 20 watts per square foot of growing area. When setting up your indoor lights, place the fluorescent tubes 6 to 12 inches above the plants' growing tips, remembering that the brightest spot under a fluorescent fixture is directly beneath the center of the tube's diameter. Shop fixtures for fluorescent tubes are often hung on chains with S-hooks to make for quick and easy adjustment. If plants are near a window, use the tubes 12 to 14 hours each day at the same time that plants receive window light.

When snipping lavender stems, be sure to cut all the way down to where the foliage begins to show. Use hand shears for the most control or hedge clippers for large plants. After harvesting each plant, cut the foliage back very severely, at least to where some yellowish leaves show. Do not, however, cut into the heavier main base stems that are woody and show no foliage or leaf buds, as new growth may not be forthcoming from these. Pruning back hard ensures that the plant doesn't get too woody and that next year's stems will be held tall and straight. Even if you don't plan to harvest the flower stems, it's still time to prune lavenders after the bloom is over.

"ladies fair, I bring to you
lavender with spikes of blue:
sweeter plant was never found
growing on our english ground."

CARYL BATTERSBY • *early-20th-century lavender brochure*

Lavender in fragrances, crafts, and cuisine

Lavender's season of bloom is so fleeting, lasting from two to six weeks for most varieties. No wonder we're drawn to cut and preserve this fragrant plant for our pleasure during the rest of the year. Fortunately, the flowers and stems of this plant readily lend themselves to drying. For quality dried flower blossoms, you'll need to take a few extra steps. Any so-called rejects from your dried flower rack can actually be used to add to potpourri mixtures or for grilling, so nothing will be wasted.

Many people forget that lavender also makes a gorgeous, scented fresh-cut flower. But cutting for fresh flower arrangements is different from cutting for dried flowers.

HARVESTING AND DRYING LAVENDER

How and when you pick lavender depends on how it will be used. For dried flowers, Jan Coello, manager of the Lavender Project (which grows 4,000 'Provence' and 'Grosso' plants for Matanzas Creek Winery near Santa Rosa, California) recommends starting to harvest for dried flowers when the lower one-third of the flowers are open and the flowers look purple. Cut with hand shears before noon on a sunny, dry day. Cutting after noon will result in wilted stems; cutting on a foggy day may lead to mildewing.

Jan Coello advises that you tie no more than 100 lavender stems in each bundle intended for drying. If you try to save effort by making the bundles any bigger, you may end up with ugly brown flower heads or moldy stems and flowers. Coello also recommends that you use rubber bands because the stems shrink as they dry and the rubber bands will maintain tension around the stems. Be aware that rubber bands can start falling apart within six months.

The single most important factor when drying lavender is to hang the bundles in a dark, dry place with plenty of good air circulation. If circulation in the drying area is poor, Coello recommends that home gardeners set up an oscillating fan and run it at low speed. She also warns that even fluorescent bulbs will fade the lavender—so keep the lavender in a dark location.

When harvesting for either fragrance or drying, Cynthia Sutphin in Massachusetts harvests the stems when the first calyxes near the bottom of the flower head begin to open. She departs from the tradition of hanging lavender bunches upside down to dry. Instead, she lays bundles of lavender stems on their sides horizontally. Sutphin thinks this makes for a more

casual American approach, as some stems dry with a weeping form, in contrast to the straight stems favored in England.

HARVESTING LAVENDER FOR POTPOURRI One of the ingredients of a good potpourri is dried lavender. For potpourri, you would follow the same instructions for harvesting and drying as above. However, no matter how tenderly you treat the crop, some flower heads will shatter while they're drying and the calyxes and corollas will fall. These fragrant parts can be collected in a sheet or tarp placed underneath the drying rack. For a potpourri enclosed in a container, you can used the shattered flower head and any full flower heads that have dried with an off color. While the color may be off on some bundles or stems, the fragrance may still abound. For a potpourri exposed in an open bowl or receptacle, you'll want to pick the best flower heads with the richest color.

HARVESTING LAVENDER FOR CULINARY USES Dried lavender is a great way to have this versatile herb available year round in the kitchen or for the grill. Since most recipes incorporate dried lavender flowers in such ways that the parts are no longer visible, saving the best colored flower heads isn't important. As for enclosed potpourri, the discolored and shattered pieces of the flower head can be used for culinary purposes. And the loose dried calyxes and any loose dried stems are good for grilling all year. Dried flower blossoms are easily substituted for dried foliage, so there's no need to dry the foliage. In most recipes, try using one-third to one-half more dried blossoms than dried leaves.

HARVESTING LAVENDER FOR FLORAL BOUQUETS The trick to harvesting lavender for any purpose is timing, and the goal when using lavender for cut-flower arrangements is to make sure it will stay fresh as long as possible. Cynthia Sutphin, proprietor of the Cape Cod Lavender Farm, that grows nearly 10,000 *Lavandula angustifolia* plants, cuts her stems for fresh bouquets while the flower buds are still tight and before the first lower calyxes have opened. If the flowers are cut when no buds are open, Sutphin notes, their stems will stay erect. A few flowers will continue to open.

Like most flowers intended for fresh bouquets, lavender should be cut early in the morning before the sun strikes the flower heads, or at least before the day gets too warm. Use a pair of bypass pruning shears (not the anvil type) with sharpened blades that will make clean, non ragged cuts. Strip off any foliage attached to the lower portion of the stems.

Once you've collected the blooms, Sutphin cautions, the stems should not be put in water. As soon as you cut the stem, it starts to turn brown. Water just speeds up the rot, and the flowers won't last. Instead, she displays her lavenders by the bunch, loading up small, attractive 4-inch-by-4-inch baskets with packed stems without using water. The lavender should remain fresh from two weeks to one month and then dry into floral arrangements that will last for years. Be sure to keep out of the direct sunlight and bright lights.

Jan Coello prefers 'Provence' for fresh flower arrangements because it maintains a straight stem, unlike 'Grosso', which in her experience droops 90 degrees just below the flower head. The 'Provence' stems are placed in water. Each day, the water is changed daily, and the bottoms of the stems are trimmed. With this care, 'Provence' remains fresh for up to 10 days. Coello also notes that if 'Provence' is placed upright in a vase or basket without water, it will dry straight and not weep.

"...we shall find a cleanly room, lavender in the windows, and twenty ballads stuck about the wall."

IZAAK WALTON • *The Compleat Angler* 1653-55

Essential Oils, Perfumes, and Toiletries

An essential oil is the concentrated volatile essence of the naturally occurring fragrant oils found in plants and flowers. Quite often, essential oils are extracted from herbs by distillation or by a process called cold-press extraction (much like that used to produce olive oil). It takes tremendous quantities of the flower, stem, bark, or foliage of some plants to make each ounce of essential oil; for example, 300 pounds of rose petals are required to produce a single fluid ounce of true rose essential oil. A true oil has not been artificially extended with alcohol, chemical fragrances, or vegetable oils.

In contrast, 4 pounds of lavandin blossoms or 8 to 16 pounds of English lavender (*L. angustifolia*) flowers will yield an ounce of essential oil. It's estimated that in the 1870s in England the production of a single pound (slightly more than 2 cups) of *L. angustifolia* lavender oil required 70 to 112 pounds of flowers and stems. Modern lavender growers in the same area now need to harvest 225 pounds of the plant for each 2 cups of lavender oil—a remarkable indication of how plant-weakening diseases have become entrenched and have lowered oil production and perhaps of how much the English weather has changed.

L. angustifolia has been the mainstay of the lavender essential-oil industry in England. The earliest mention of lavender growing in England occurred in 1301, as reported in the records of the Merton Prioiry (like a parish or borough), as a way to raise money to lend to King Edward I. The earliest recorded cultivation of lavender for commerce was in the late 1700s by the Mitcham (also a district, parish, or borough) farmers on the outskirts of London, England. The English lavender–oil industry has waned considerably since its prime in the mid to late 1800s. In 1982 the largest planting of lavender in England was a mere 90 acres, and England has actually become an importer of lavender oil. The true English product is still available, but at a premium price, and essential oil from *L. angustifolia* is now produced not only in England but also in France, Bulgaria, the Netherlands, and China, and even in small quantities in the United States.

The oil that has come to dominate the world supply—especially for use in the detergent and soap industries—is often dubbed French lavender oil, but is more properly labeled lavandin oil. Although some lavandin oil comes from France, it is produced by a natural interspecific hybrid of English lavender (*L. angustifolia*) and spike lavender (*L. latifolia*), and is not to be confused with English lavender oil (from *L. angustifolia* alone)—the standard for sweet, fresh -smelling, and delicate oil characteristics.

The lavandin hybrid was developed as a means of circumventing the diseases affecting certain varieties of English lavender and of increasing the amount of oil yielded by an acre's worth of harvested stems and blossoms (the leaves are not used for distillation). English lavender may yield up to 2 gallons of oil per acre. Lavandin can produce 7 to 11 gallons of oil per acre—in other words, about four times the amount produced by English lavender.

ESSENTIAL DETAILS ABOUT LAVENDER OIL

Lavender oil is a concentrated herbal extract and, that being the case, is not completely benign. According to some sources, pure lavender oil is hypo-allergenic (this does not necessarily apply to preparations made with small amounts of the oil combined with other ingredients). Cases of dermatitis from use of the pure oil have been reported, however, and lavender bath preparations have caused skin inflammation. Some handbooks for the medicinal-herb industry list lavender oil as a "narcotic poison" that can cause death by convulsions, but *very* large doses—far more than the recommended limit of two drops of essential oil at one time—are required to achieve this effect. The concentrated vapors from the oil, if breathed for too long a time, have been known to cause a form of intoxication, with symptoms of nausea, vomiting, headache, and chills. Prudence suggests, therefore, that the first time you use pure lavender oil externally, test it on a small patch of skin. Herbalists also recommend that you never take more than two drops of this essential oil internally at one time.

In summary, in the pursuit of tougher plants and greater yields of oil, the quality of the "French" or lavandin essential oil has suffered. Lavandin, by all accountings, is less sweet, slightly more astringent, and slightly harsher than English lavender oil made from *L. angustifolia*. The differences are subtle enough, however, that many people can't tell the difference, even in a side-by-side sniff or taste test.

Lavadin may contain up to 12 percent camphor, while English lavender contains less than 1 percent camphor, thus its relatively sweeter fragrance and flavor. Because it yields high amounts of oil per acre, the lavandin cultivar 'Grosso' now dominates the laundry, detergent, and soap lavender industries.

The above suggests why some true lavender oils can cost more than lavandin oil.

Since the production of essential oil is impractical for most gardeners, the natural scent of the flower and foliage becomes a dominant factor in the choice and appreciation of a plant.

Other than taking on the difficult task of discovering new oil-rich hybrids or seedlings, there is little one can do to increase the essential oil content of lavender. The exception is to use a 1-inch-thick mulch of white sand (not salty beach sand) around lavender plants. As mentioned earlier, research done by Drs. Arthur Tucker, John Howell, and Michael Maciarello in Delaware suggests that a sand mulch improves the oil content of lavender foliage from 28 percent to a staggering 771 percent. The higher the oil content of the foliage, the greater the potential for aroma and flavor.

BLENDING ESSENTIAL OILS

Essential oils may be used alone or combined with others to create a personalized blend. *L. angustifolia* combines aptly with bergamot, clary sage, geranium, lemon, patchouli, pine, rose, and rosemary. Lavandins blend well with any of these oils and also with citronella, cinnamon, clove, cypress, marjoram, melissa, lemongrass, juniper berry, and thyme.

Since essential oils can be rather intense and, like lavender, can cause dermatitis, another, more gentle oil is generally used as an extending agent or carrier to dilute the essential concentrate. Good carrier oils include sweet almond, peach kernel, soya, sesame, jojoba, coconut, and grapeseed. Lavender oil can be used alone in a carrier oil or blended "to taste" with other essential oils. Some essential oils evaporate very quickly; to extend the life of the fragrance, an extender or fixative is added to the oil. Common extenders and fixatives for lavender are orris root (made from special iris rhizomes), calamus root (the rhizome, also called sweet sedge, is used and grows in moist soils), and storax (from the bark of *Styrax officinalis*).

By definition, there are natural perfumes and synthetic (artificial or chemical) perfumes. Natural perfumes are of animal or vegetable origin, such as the blended essential oils mentioned above, and may be mixed with alcohol in order to create a commercial perfume. Synthetic perfumes are chemical compounds made to mimic natural scents; examples of such chemical counterfeits are most vanillin extracts and many so-called lavender perfumes.

Lavender oil is one of the world's most popular choices for blending into natural perfumes or for mimicking in artificial fragrances. As the costs of lavender cultivation and distillation have risen, the use of synthetic, chemically produced "clones" of lavender have skyrocketed. The nose of the average perfume shopper will not be able to distinguish the subtle differences between a true essential oil and an artificial lavender scent, so lavender aficionados who want the real thing need to research sources of lavender oils and perfumes in order to determine their trustworthiness and honesty.

If you wish to concoct your own lavender perfumes, it's helpful to know a small amount of fragrance chemistry. Each pure, unadulterated essential oil in a perfume blend adds one "note." The "top" note or notes in a perfume create the smell you first perceive as the fragrance dissipates, meaning the aroma is the quickest to evaporate. The "middle" or "body" note or notes are the second scent to dissipate. The final aroma that emerges as the fragrance begins to dry out is termed the "low" or "base" note or notes. As with music, the blending of perfumes means assembling combinations of all these "notes" in order to compose a complete "symphony." The notes of a manufactured fragrance can be revealed by dipping a stick into it and observing each scent that emerges as the perfume dries. Lavandin and *L. angustifolia* oils are used to produce both the top and the middle notes of many a celebrated fragrance.

When creating your perfume blends, remember that because essential oils don't dissolve in water but just float on top, you'll need to use alcohol as a dissolving medium. Many perfume blends contain pharmaceutical-grade alcohol (90 to 95 percent alcohol, available at the local pharmacy) with 12 to 30 percent essential oil, or 100-proof vodka (50 percent alcohol) combined with 5 percent essential oil. (By comparison, a cologne or toilet water contains about 85 percent alcohol, 11 percent water, and 3 to 4 percent essential oil.)

Here's one of thousands of essential oil blends that can be turned into a lavender-based perfume, this one distinguished by a sweet floral aroma with evocative light citrus notes.

2 drops of lemon essential oil (top note)

6 drops of lavender essential oil (middle or top note)

5 drops of sandalwood essential oil (base note)

Add to ½ ounce pharmaceutical-grade alcohol or ¾ ounce 100-proof vodka (makes a slightly weaker perfume). Adjust to suit your senses.

Let's not forget the medicinal properties of aromatic oil. Try this massage oil for back pain. Add to 1 tablespoon of carrier oil, such as sweet almond, peach kernel, or grapeseed:

7 drops lavender essential oil

5 drops ginger essential oil

5 drops eucalyptus essential oil

Since the average gardener can't make his or her own essential oil, it's best to purchase essential oils from a health food store; a complete herbal supply store; a shop featuring aromatherapy supplies; one of the large full-service, organic grocery stores; or a mail-order outlet for herbs, aromatherapy supplies, and essential oils. The sources at the end of the book provide addresses for mail-order suppliers.

"And lavender, whose spikes of azure bloom
shall be, ere-while, in arid bundles bound
to lurk admist the labours of her loom,
and crown her kerchiefs with mickle rare perfume."

WILLIAM SHENSTONE • *The School Mistress* 1742

Toiletries

The oldest and perhaps most frequently used lavender product is the preparation known as lavender water. Recipes for this simple, soothing potion were exchanged by women of the Roman Empire and for centuries were common in the household books of good homemakers throughout Europe and Colonial America. Lavender water can provide a refreshing splash or spray of delicate fragrance for the face, hands, or body. It's especially delightful when chilled for relief from the heat on a hot summer day.

This soothing toiletry is easy to brew, but as with so much lavender lore, its name is deceptive, since no actual water is involved. To concoct lavender water, begin with a clean, clear glass jar. Fill the jar loosely with 3 to 4 ounces of flower heads per quart of liquid, which should be 90-proof brandy or vodka, rather than water. Add the liquid, let the flowers steep in the sun for a few days, strain, add more flowers, repeat the steeping, and so on, until the lavender scent is to your liking. Lavender water has traditionally been used for anointing weak, brittle, or falling-out hair several times per week, for treating rheumatic joints, for dabbing on the temples to soothe headaches, for splashing on the skin as a refresher, or as a perfume. Since concentrated lavender can produce uncomfortable side effects, herbal wisdom strongly advises against taking this concoction internally.

"...his aunt jobiska made him drink
lavender water tinged with pink,
    for she said, 'the world in general knows
        there's nothing so good for a pobble's toes!'"

EDWARD LEAR • *"The Pobble Who has No Toes" from* Laughable Lyrics

Lavender maintains a long-lived and well-deserved reputation for having a calming, relaxing effect on people and animals. Perhaps the popularity of lavender fragrance lies in its supposed ability (in the language of aromatherapy) to balance, relax, gently clarify, restore, uplift, normalize, invigorate, and soothe mind, body, and spirit. Whether this herbal lore is fact or fiction is irrelevant when you're luxuriating in a tub perfumed by a sweet diffusion of lavender vapors.

For an utterly relaxing experience, try this mineral-bath recipe, provided by *Aromatherapy Notes*, published by the Aura Cacia Company. Citrus oils are reputed to be uplifting, so if you want more of a soothing effect, reduce the citrus oils and increase the lavender oil. Combine the ingredients, then add to a hot bath.

3 tablespoons sea salt   *5 drops lemon essential oil*
2 tablespoons baking soda   *7 drops lavender essential oil*
1 tablespoon borax   *2 drops chamomile essential oil*
6 drops tangerine essential oil

Here's another bathing mixture from Aura Cacia. Mix the oils, then use 5 to 10 drops per hot bath.

1 drop juniper berry oil   *7 drops bergamot essential oil*
1 drop patchouli essential oil   *7 drops lavender essential oil*

Whether these wonderful-smelling preparations have any true physiological impact is yet to be proven conclusively, but as hedonistic and sensual experiences go, they're difficult to top.

Potpourris and Crafts

A potpourri is a mixture of dried herbs, spices, flowers and fruit peels, to which essential oils may be added. Such a mixture was traditionally thought not only to freshen the air, but to lift the spirits. Potpourris have a long history of use, especially in times before the invention of modern air fresheners, when the air in a home might otherwise smell of farm animals, sewage, kerosene lamps, coal-fired furnaces, or other pollutants. Even with all the modern alternatives to potpourris, there's something incomparably charming and evocative about an open bowl of colorful dried herbs, spices, and flowers placed on a table or windowsill, slowly filling the room with a sweet, elaborate aroma.

Dried lavender blossoms, because of their lasting fragrance, are one of the most common ingredients in the multitude of mixtures defined as potpourris. Here's a simple starter mix that makes about 3¾ cups.

1 to 2 cups dried lavender flowers
¼ to ½ cup dried marjoram leaves
¾ cup dried rose petals
¼ cup dried mint

¼ cup dried thyme leaves
1 tablespoon grated dried orange peel
¼ teaspoon ground cloves
¼ teaspoon ground cinnamon

Mix the dried herbs and flowers, and store them in a glass or earthenware jar for a month or more, shaking or stirring often. Make sure the lid seals tightly so the aromas mingle and remain in the jar. If you want more herbal intensity, you can add a few drops of lavender essential oil to this recipe. Many other potpourri recipes can be found in books about herbs, or you may wish to experiment, using the above method, with various combinations of plants from your own yard.

Lavender has a long history in herbal lore as a cure for insomnia, and modern herbalists have touted the lavender pillow as a remedy for sleeplessness, colds, flu, bronchitis, and tonsillitis. A study in France titled "Neurodepressive effects of the essential oil of *Lavandula angustifolia*" found that oil of lavender had a sedative effect on mice. An earlier study by the same researchers found that the essential oil of lavender relieved anxiety in mice (whatever mice worry about) and prolonged drug-induced sleeping time—but only for the first five days after it was given. So, science marches on, one step forward and one step back, attempting to keep up with the folk wisdom that has dictated the creation and use of lavender pillows for centuries.

To create your own lavender pillow, make a muslin, cotton, or silk pillowcasing of any shape, often a small elongated rectangle to place over the eyes or to be tucked under the neck. It can be filled with lavender flower buds (calyxes). More complex mixtures use three parts of dried lavender flowers to one part each of hop flowers (also reputed to help with insomnia), dried rosemary leaves, dried marjoram leaves, and dried sweet cicely leaves. To a well-blended mix of these components, you may add several drops of lavender essential oil and stir again. You can also blend in an equal amount of flaxseed to add weight and a smooth texture to a pillow meant to be placed over the eyes.

LAVENDER WANDS

Lavender is wonderful for scenting drawers full of underwear, sweaters, or linens and other bedding. A delightful alternative to sachets, made by tying or sewing the loose herb into bags, is the lavender wand, also called a lavender bottle—the more common term in England. A finished lavender wand has a gentle, curved oval shape or a fat, squatty rotund form, depending upon the number and size of the flowerheads contained within the wand. This ingenious craft is superior to a sachet in that it allows closer contact with the fragrance of the herb itself, but contains the mess as the heads shatter from drying. The wand will scent a drawer for up to a decade.

In making a lavender wand, it's important to follow these step-by-step directions.

- Cut 20, 22, 24, or 26 stems of lavender. The stems need to be at least twice the length of the flower heads—the longer the better. The number of stems used depends upon how large the flower heads are; the fatter the flower head, the fewer stems are needed. Be sure to cut from varieties with long stems—lavandins such as 'Provence' and 'Grosso', *L. latifolia*, *L. heterophylla* or some of the bigger species form of *L. angustifolia*. Strip the stems of all leaves.

- Using one end of a ½-inch-wide ribbon 24 to 36 inches long, tie all the stems together just below the flower heads.

- Bend each stem back and away from the center of the bunch at the point where it's tied and bring loosely over the flower heads. When you're finished, the flower heads will be encased in an encircling "cage" of stems. Tie the stems together loosely near the ends with a short piece of string.

- Hang each "cage" from the string attached to the stems, and dry for one to two weeks. This initial drying allows some shrinkage, so the fully dried wand won't have gaps in the ribbon that let the dried calyxes fall out.

- After one to two weeks, untie the string from the stems so that the stems spread out from the center. Take the long free section of ribbon in one hand and bring it out from the center, passing it through the splayed-out stems at any point. Take two stems either to the right or left of the ribbon, and lace the ribbon over these two stems—perpendicular to their lengths— as closely as possible to the tip of the forming bottled-shaped "cage." Lace the ribbon under the next two stems, and continue this weaving pattern until all the flower heads are encased within a stem-and-ribbon "cage." After lacing over or under each set of two stems, be sure to pull the ribbon snug, drawing the stems together and making sure that the edges of the ribbon weave are as close together as possible. As you lace over and under the double stems, the stems and the ribbon will encase the flower heads.

- When the ribbon has been woven just beyond the flower heads, wrap it around the outside of all the stems very tightly three or four times, and tie it off with a bow.

Cooking with Lavender

Virtually all parts of a lavender shrub growing above ground have culinary uses. Some parts, such as the corollas, are sweeter. Other parts, as with the twigs and stems, are too bitter for dessert recipes but make a savory smoke for grilling.

Lavender flowers can be used in many appetizers, entrées, and desserts. The sweetest and most aromatic lavender desserts are those made with the true flower petals, or corollas, as opposed to the entire flower head; this is because the latter includes more woody parts and fewer of the pure, subtle-flavored petals of the former. Since the oil-exuding glands in the woody parts of the flower head discharge more of the plant's camphor and resinous compounds than do those of the calyxes and corollas, recipes using the entire flower will be a bit more astringent and a touch less sweet. You can make your recipe sweeter by not using the stems; they are even more bitter and harsh than the woody parts of the flower.

The lavender foliage, though much more pungent than the flowers and thus not as appropriate for ice cream, sorbets, or other delicate desserts, is a delicious cooking ingredient in its own right. Fresh foliage is also much more available during the growing year than the blossoms. In mild climates, such as Zones 8, 9, 10, and 11, the foliage is in good shape for harvest throughout the year. In colder zones, such as Zone 5, the foliage may not be useful as a fresh ingredient from late fall until early spring, but may be dried for winter use. Using the foliage of lavender in addition to its flowers certainly extends the culinary "season" for this unique herb.

The lavender stems are much woodier than the foliage or flower heads, and are nowhere near as tasty, but they do provide a great source of aromatic smoke for grilling and smoking meats, vegetables, and fish.

Though all varieties of lavender stems can be used to smoke food, the stems of lavandin lavenders are especially recommended. They are longer than those of most other species and are easier to clean, and their smoke imparts a complex lavender flavor to whatever is being grilled. Save the long stems after the flower heads have fully dried, and remove any leaf or flower remnants. The stems can be thrown on the hot coals of an outdoor grill to infuse a lavender taste into food via the smoke.

Lavender foliage can be used in sweet desserts for much of the year, but since it is much stronger in flavor than the flowers, it should be used in much smaller amounts. Try using foliage in amounts one-half to one-third of the quantity of flowers called for in a recipe. Reduce the amount further in subsequent versions of the recipe if the flavor turns out too robust. For use in desserts, the foliage may be chopped, added to any previously measured amount of granulated sugar called for in the recipe, and blended to a fine mixture in a food processor.

If you have used dried flowers for a recipe and switch to fresh flowers and foliage, use one-third to one-half more fresh flowers or fresh leaf. If it's winter and you have only dried lavender flowers and the recipe calls for fresh flowers or foliage, use one-third to one-half less dried flowers.

Any recipe that calls for the herb rosemary (*Rosmarinus officinalis*) can be turned into a lavender recipe by the substitution of fresh lavender foliage for fresh rosemary. Rosemary is very popular for cooking throughout the world, especially in the Mediterranean region, and, like lavender, belongs to the *Labiatae*, or mint, family. Its leaves have a pungent, resinous, and intense flavor that is far more powerful than that of lavender foliage, so more lavender must be used to obtain an equal intensity. Here are two basic guidelines for substituting fresh lavender for fresh rosemary.

•   In a recipe that includes sugar, use two times more finely chopped lavender foliage than the specified amount of finely chopped rosemary leaves.

•   In any recipe that combines rosemary with liquids (water, broth, fruit juice, etc.), try using—by volume—three or four times more finely chopped lavender foliage than rosemary. The finer you chop the foliage, the more the aromatic, savory oils will be released.

As a basis for experimenting with lavender foliage, here's a list of recipes and foods commonly seasoned with rosemary.

baked beans

bread and biscuits

citrus: grapefruits and oranges

cheese (soft)

fish and seafood

fritters

jellies and conserves

meat: beef, lamb, mutton, pork, and roast pork

mushrooms

poultry: chicken, duck, partridge, pheasant, and turkey

salads and salad dressings

soups: chicken, tomato, and vegetable

stews: beef and lamb

vegetables: cauliflower, garlic, onions, potatoes, shallots, spinach, and zucchini

vinegars

Makes about ¾ cup

Makes 2 dozen crystallized flowers

A common mixture in the Provence district of France includes the crushed dried foliage or flowers of basil, marjoram, parsley, thyme, and lavender in a combination known as herbes de Provence. These blends come in as many forms as there are family names in Provence; some actually exclude lavender, but all of the true or older blends contain this sweet floral ingredient. This is one of the hundreds of possible recipes for herbes de Provence. As did the originators of this form of culinary expression, feel free to experiment with the proportions and ingredients. Use to season vegetables, poultry, or red meats.

3 tablespoons dried lavender flowers
3 tablespoons dried marjoram or
*   oregano leaves*
3 tablespoons dried thyme leaves
3 tablespoons dried savory leaves
1 teaspoon dried rosemary leaves
1 teaspoon dried basil leaves
½ teaspoon dried sage leaves

Combine all the ingredients in a small jar with a tight-fitting lid and mix well. Store in a dark, cool place. The mixture will keep for years, but is best used within one year.

One of the easiest transformations for lavender is the crystallizing of its flowers to be used as cake and pastry decorations or nibbled like candy. Because of the fragrant oils contained in lavender flowers, each separate candied calyx with its corolla becomes, in effect, a tiny lavender-flavored breath freshener. Leave the heads on the stems to make drying easier.

2 dozen fresh lavender flower heads
1 egg white
¼ cup confectioner's sugar or superfine sugar

Pick the flowering heads when they are about 50 percent open, leaving stems 4 to 6 inches long. Let any surface moisture evaporate from the heads if they aren't already dry.

Whisk the egg white lightly in a small bowl. Using a small watercolor brush, apply a thin coating of egg white to all surfaces of each flower head, making sure to rub it between and around the individual calyxes.

Push a drinking straw into the confectioner's or superfine sugar and use it to blow the sugar over each egg-white-coated flower head as you rotate the stem between your index finger and thumb. Alternatively, gently tap a spoonful of sugar above the flower head to achieve the same effect. Repeat once or twice to coat all flower surfaces evenly, but don't apply so much sugar that the color of the blossom begins to fade.

Set each flower stem upright in a piece of plastic foam to allow the egg whites to dry thoroughly. This sugaring process will preserve the blossoms for years. Store the crystallized flower heads in a lidded jar.

Whether you like to sip a drink while cooking, or surprise your guests with unusual spirits before, during, or after a meal, lavender can add a zesty and unusual flavor to classic beverages:

LAVENDER WINE

The simplest of all. Just pluck 4 to 10 lavender corollas from a fresh flower head and let them skate across your favorite white wine in a chilled glass. Or simply put a stem with a small flower head into the glass with the stem delicately lying over the rim like an upside-down swizzle stick.

LAVENDER MARTINI

To your favorite martini recipe, add a small flower head of lavender as a garnish; the lavender oil is quickly and subtly released by the alcohol. For a stiffer lavender flavor, shake or stir your martini with one *small* drop of lavender essential oil, and float a few lavender corollas across the top of the drink.

Salute!

This is based on an idea originally found in THE FORGOTTEN ART OF FLOWER COOKERY, *by Leona Woodring Smith.*

Makes 3 pints

This recipe comes from Jerry Traunfeld of The Herbfarm in Fall City, Washington. Since plums begin to ripen at the same time as the lavender blooms, these two crops are a natural culinary pairing. Spread this chutney on a turkey sandwich, use it as an appetizer on crackers with blue cheese, or enjoy it with entrées featuring grilled pork or chicken.

> *5 pounds nearly ripe red or purple plums*
> *1 medium onion, finely chopped*
> *Grated zest and juice of 2 lemons*
> *1½ tablespoons chopped fresh ginger*
> *1 tablespoon whole yellow mustard seed*
> *1 teaspoon hot red pepper flakes*
> *¼ cup sherry vinegar*
> *¾ cup firmly-packed brown sugar*
> *½ teaspoon salt*
> *1½ tablespoons chopped fresh lavender*
>   *flower heads*

Cut the plums in half, remove the pits, and slice the fruit into ½-inch wedges. Place in a heavy-bottomed saucepan and add the onion, lemon zest and juice, ginger, mustard seed, red pepper flakes, vinegar, brown sugar, and salt. Bring the mixture to a boil, then turn the heat to low and simmer, stirring often, until very thick, about 45 minutes.

Stir in the lavender. Pack the chutney in sterilized 1-pint or 8-ounce jars and seal according to the manufacturer's directions. The chutney will keep indefinitely. Or, cool the chutney and store in the refrigerator for up to one month.

Serves 6 to 8

This recipe, although it may look complicated, is quite a simple salad, and one that serves up as an elegant lunch or a cool dinner on a blazing-hot summer night. Tamara Frey, a professional chef who lives in a hot-summer California valley, uses the wines from her family's organic vineyard, one of the first in the United States.

For the vinaigrette:
    ½ cup extra-virgin olive oil
    3 tablespoons late-harvest sauvignon blanc
    2 tablespoons raspberry vinegar
    1 teaspoon minced fresh lavender leaves
    2 tablespoons lime juice
    Salt and pepper to taste

For the marinade:
    ¼ cup late-harvest sauvignon blanc
    2 teaspoons minced fresh lavender leaves
    2 tablespoons raspberry vinegar
    2 tablespoons lime juice
    2 tablespoons extra virgin olive oil
    Salt and pepper to taste

For the salad:
    1 pound salmon fillet
    1 tablespoon extra-virgin olive oil
    2 bunches spinach
    1 cucumber, peeled and sliced
    1 avocado, peeled, pitted, and sliced
    1 red onion thinly sliced
    1 cup raspberries or 2 kiwi fruits,
       peeled and sliced, for garnish

To prepare the vinaigrette, combine all of the ingredients in a jar with a tight-fitting lid, and shake until blended. Taste and adjust the seasonings. Set aside.

To prepare the marinade, combine all of the ingredients in a small bowl.

To prepare the salad, make sure the salmon is free of bones. Place it in a bowl and add the marinade. Cover and marinate for 1 hour in the refrigerator, turning the fillet every 15 minutes. Remove the salmon and reserve the marinade.

Heat olive oil in a sauté pan over medium heat and sauté the salmon filet on both sides approximately 5 minutes. Pour the reserved marinade over the salmon and simmer until the marinade thickens into a sauce, about 2 to 4 minutes. Remove the salmon to a plate with a slotted spoon, and gently flake it into small pieces. Return to the pan and toss gently with the sauce.

Remove the stems from the spinach and divide among 6 to 8 plates. Place the salmon in the center of the spinach and pour the additional sauce over the salmon. Arrange the sliced cucumber, avocado, red onion, and raspberries or kiwi slices around the salmon. Sprinkle with vinaigrette and serve.

Serves 6 to 8

"Pressada," a coined term for chicken pressed between two layers of lavender, is based on a dish made with thyme that I enjoyed in Italy, south of Naples. This is a true gardener's recipe because few nongardeners could afford to buy the amount of fresh lavender required. The quick-cooking chicken first steams between two layers of freshly cut lavender. Then the cooked chicken is stripped of lavender and quickly browned on a grill. Serve the chicken on rice pilaf or a bed of colorful mesclun.

While you are eating, you can add the leftover lavender foliage to the coals to produce a heady lavender fragrance.

6 to 8 chicken breasts or other cuts, bones and skin removed
Olive oil for brushing
5-gallon bucket loosely filled with fresh lavender foliage and flower stalks

Light a fire in a charcoal grill. Meanwhile, rinse the chicken parts thoroughly under cold running water and pat dry. Once the flames are out and the coals are white at the edges, arrange the coals in a uniform layer. Place the grill rack over the coals and set a 10-inch-by-20-inch cast-iron pancake griddle on top of the rack. The griddle should be directly above—less than ½ inch—the hot coals. Heat the griddle until it is nearly orange-hot. When oil dropped on the griddle dances and sizzles, you're ready to begin.

Quickly coat the griddle with the olive oil, which prevents the herbs from sticking and makes cleaning easier. Don't use a brush with plastic bristles as the intense heat of the metal will melt the bristles.

Working quickly, layer up to 2 inches of lavender foliage on the griddle with the stems all running in one direction. Be sure to cover the griddle thoroughly with the lavender and leave no holes. Lay the chicken on top of the lavender, with the lengths of the pieces perpendicular to the lengths of lavender. Cover the chicken thoroughly with another 2 inches of lavender foliage. Set a baking sheet on top of the chicken-and-lavender "sandwich." Stack 5-10 bricks evenly on top of the baking sheet to compress the lavender and chicken (the "pressada" part).

Because the heat supercharges the volatile essential oils in the lavender, the resulting steam and oil mixture quickly cooks the chicken. The chicken may need only 5 to 10 minutes per side if the griddle was nearly orange-hot, 15 to 20 minutes per side if the charcoal wasn't hot enough.

When the chicken is done—a knife score shows only white flesh—on one side, remove the bricks and the baking sheet and use tongs to turn the entire sandwich as quickly as possible. The lavender and chicken will usually hold together enough to allow you to turn them as a unified whole. You'll either amaze your guests or have to reassemble the lavender-and-chicken sandwich while eating humble pie. Practice makes perfect.

When the chicken is juicy but no pink flesh shows when meat is tested with a knife, remove the bricks and baking sheet and the top layer of lavender foliage. Lift the chicken off the bottom layer of foliage, and place on a platter. Then remove the lavender and the griddle from the grill rack. Quickly restoke the coals and place the chicken pieces on the grill rack, setting them at a diagonal to the lines of the rack. Briefly brown the chicken on both sides. Transfer to a serving platter.

Serves 4

Makes 2 loaves

This is a fabulous treat from Ditty Deamer. She says this quick and supremely simple main dish will make your guests wonder if you have a secret source for lavender-fed lamb. A hearty meal for the winter months.

Hot, home-baked bread is one of life's true comfort foods. Why not make it even more comforting with a touch of lavender? This recipe is provided by John Mancarella, owner of The Belmont in Belmont, Maine.

1 tablespoon olive oil
Small handful of young fresh lavender sprigs
(leaves and flowers), cut long enough to
span the diameter of a sauté pan
4 whole cloves garlic, peeled and lightly
smashed with a cleaver or heavy knife
4 small rib lamb chops, ¾ inch thick,
trimmed of fat
Salt and pepper to taste

1 cup lukewarm water (about 120° F)
3¾ teaspoons active dry yeast
(about 1½ packages)
1 cup buttermilk
⅓ cup olive oil
¼ cup fresh lavender leaves, finely chopped
1 tablespoon plus 1 teaspoon salt
6¾ cups all-purpose flour
Yellow cornmeal for sprinkling baking sheet
Coarse salt for sprinkling loaves

Add olive oil to the bottom of a sauté pan large enough to hold the lamb chops in one layer. Add the lavender sprigs and garlic cloves and set over high heat.

Place the chops in the sauté pan on top of the lavender and garlic and sear both sides, then lower the heat to medium and cook them for 2 minutes on each side. This timing will result in relatively pink meat, but cook the chops longer if they are thicker than ¾ inch or if you prefer the meat well done. Turn off the heat, cover the pan, and allow the chops to sit for 3 to 4 minutes. This gives the cooking juices time to continue cooking the chops without direct heat, which enhances the succulence of the meat.

Season with salt and pepper to taste. Serve with sprigs of the browned lavender and garlic as a fragrant, edible garnish.

Place the lukewarm water in a large bowl and stir in the yeast. Let stand until foamy, about 10 minutes.

Add the buttermilk, olive oil, lavender, and salt, and mix until well blended. Add the flour gradually, beating slowly until each addition is incorporated. Continue blending until the dough is elastic. Turn the dough onto a floured work surface, and knead dough until smooth and elastic, about 2 minutes. Add just enough flour to keep the bread from being too sticky to handle.

Place the dough in a lightly oiled bowl, turn to coat it evenly with oil, and let it rise, covered with plastic wrap, in a warm place until doubled in bulk, about 1½ hours.

Turn the dough onto a floured work surface and knead it for 2 to 3 minutes. Cut in half. Shape each half into a round and place both portions on a baking sheet that has been lightly oiled and sprinkled with cornmeal. Cover the loaves with a

continued

dampened kitchen towel and let rise for 1 hour.

Place a rack in the middle of an oven and preheat the oven to 425° F. With a serrated knife, gently cut a large asterisk shape into the top of each loaf, and sprinkle with coarse salt.

Bake the loaves until they are golden and their bottoms sound hollow when tapped, about 55 minutes. During the first 15 minutes, spray them occasionally with water, which gives the loaves a hard crust. Transfer the loaves to racks to cool completely.

LAVENDER-LEMON SHORTBREAD

Makes 12 shortbread cookies

Shortbread came originally from the British Isles, and cooks in England, Scotland, and Ireland all passed down family recipes through the generations. Combining the simple flavors of butter, sugar, and flour, the cookies are just barely sweet, but quite addictive. The shortbread pairs the classic flavors of lemon, lavender, and butter to make a fancy cookie that will class up a simple dessert of fruit. Jeff Dawson, a gardener and writer from Sebastopol, California, passed on this recipe from chef Tess McDonough of Kendall Jackson Winery.

1 cup unsalted butter, at room temperature
1 cup sugar
2 teaspoons grated lemon zest
¼ teaspoon salt
3 cups flour
2 teaspoons lavender calyxes, dried and
   removed from the stems

Preheat an oven to 325° F.

In a large bowl, beat the butter, sugar, and lemon zest with an electric mixer or by hand until just blended; do not overbeat. Sift the flour and lavender calyxes into a bowl, rubbing the buds through the sieve with your hand.

Slowly add the lavender flour and salt to the butter and sugar, mixing until just incorporated. Scrape down the sides of the bowl if necessary in order to blend all of the ingredients, being careful not to overbeat.

Press the resulting dough firmly into a 10-inch springform pan or pie tin. Pierce the dough in a few places with a fork to prevent it from bubbling and to allow excess steam to be released. Score or perforate the dough to make cutting the wedges easier after baking.

Bake until golden brown around the edges, 25 to 35 minutes. Let cool for 2 minutes. With a knife, cut the shortbread round into 12 wedges. When the pieces are completely cool, carefully remove from the pan. Store in an airtight container.

Serves about 8

A classic summertime treat to beat the heat. Crank up the ice cream maker during aperitifs so the ice cream can cure during dinner. Chef, owner of Restaurant Nora in Washington, D.C., and food consultant Nora Pouillon graciously provided the recipe for this delicious dessert treat.

> *3 cups heavy cream*
> *2 tablespoons fresh lavender flowers*
> *½ cup sugar*
> *½ cup water*
> *3 egg yolks*
> *Crystallized Lavender Flowers for garnish*
>   *(see page 101)*

Heat the cream in a saucepan. Add the lavender flowers and bring to a boil while stirring constantly. Set aside.

In a small bowl, combine the sugar and the water, and stir to dissolve the sugar. Pour mixture into a small saucepan and bring to a boil. Boil for about 10 minutes, until it reaches 220° F on a candy thermometer. (Do not touch or stir the sugar while it's boiling. If sugar crystals form on the side of the pan, the syrup will crystallize.) Set aside.

Place egg yolks in a bowl and, using a whisk or an electric mixer, whip until they are yellow and fluffy, about 5 minutes. Carefully pour the hot sugar syrup down the inside of the bowl. Whip for about 1 minute without spattering the syrup. Add lavender cream and beat until combined. Strain this custard to remove the bits of lavender, cover with plastic wrap, and refrigerate until cool. Pour into an ice-cream maker and freeze.

Serves 4

This cooling dessert is an oasis in the middle of steaming hot-summer days, but its delicate flavors can also be appreciated in winter. This dish makes an effective palette cleanser between courses. Blood oranges are usually available only during the winter months. Mimi Luebbermann, cookbook and garden book author, suggests using the sugar-lavender syrup with any fresh-cut fruit.

> *2 pink grapefruits*
> *2 blood or navel oranges*
> *1 white grapefruit*
> *½ cup sugar*
> *½ cup water*
> *2 tablespoons lavender calyxes*
> *Lemon sorbet*
> *Raspberry sorbet*

With a paring knife, peel grapefruits and oranges, removing both the peel and the white pith. Working over a bowl, cut out fruit sections by using the knife to free sections from the membranes. Let the sections drop into bowl and squeeze any remaining juice from the membranes into the bowl.

Place the sugar, water, and lavender calyxes in a small saucepan and gradually bring to a low simmer. Simmer the sauce 3 to 4 minutes. Add juice from the reserved fruit into the saucepan. Taste the sauce: if you wish a stronger lavender flavor, simmer for a few more minutes. Remove the sauce from the heat and drain into the fruit through a fine-mesh sieve to remove the lavender. Chill until ready to serve.

To serve, divide the fruit between 4 dessert bowls. Add to each bowl a small scoop of raspberry sorbet and a small scoop of lemon sorbet. Serve immediately.

LAVENDER BUNDT CAKE

Serves 12 to 14

This airy, light sponge cake has lavender through-out. Coralie Castle, who created this recipe, has an extensive background in cooking with flowers and has been publishing cookbooks since 1972.

> *1 cup unsalted butter, at room temperature*
> *2⅔ cups sifted unbleached all-purpose flour*
> *½ teaspoon rose water*
> *½ teaspoon vanilla extract*
> *4 tablespoons chopped fresh lavender flowers*
> *1 teaspoon freshly grated orange zest*
> *8 egg whites, at room temperature*
> *¼ teaspoon salt*
> *¼ teaspoon cream of tartar*
> *1⅔ cups Granulated Lavender Sugar*
> *Lavender Confectioner's Sugar*
> *Crystallized Lavender Flowers (page 101)*

Preheat an oven to 350° F. Butter a 10-inch bundt pan and dust with flour; set aside.

In a large bowl, using a wooden spoon or an elec-tric mixer, beat the butter until creamy. Gradually add 1⅓ cups of the flour, beating until the mixture is smooth and fluffy. Stir in the rose water, vanilla, lavender, and orange zest.

In a medium bowl, combine the egg whites, salt, and cream of tartar, and beat until soft peaks form. Continuing to beat, add the Granulated Lavender Sugar, 1 tablespoon at a time. Beat until the mixture is smooth and glossy, about 3 minutes.

Stir one-fourth of the egg whites into the butter mixture to lighten it, then fold in the remaining egg whites. Sift the remaining 1⅓ cups flour over the batter, a little at a time, and gently fold in to incorporate. Don't overmix.

Pour the batter into the prepared pan and bake until the cake pulls away from the pan sides and a toothpick inserted in the center comes out clean and golden brown, about 50 minutes.

Remove the cake to a rack and let cool for 15 to 20 minutes. Turn out onto the rack, invert, and let cool completely. Wrap in plastic wrap and let stand 24 hours before slicing.

Before serving, sift Lavender Confectioner's Sugar over the cake, garnish with candied lavender flowers.

LAVENDER GRANULATED SUGAR

Makes 1⅔ cups

> *1⅔ cups granulated sugar*
> *4 to 6 flower heads of English lavender, minced*

Pound and combine the sugar and minced flowers in a mortar with a pestle, or process in a food processor. Place in a well-sealed jar for at least one week before using. The sugar keeps for about three months.

LAVENDER CONFECTIONER'S SUGAR

Makes 1⅔ cups

> *1⅔ cups confectioner's sugar*
> *2 to 3 flower heads of English lavender, minced*

Mix the confectioner's sugar with the minced lavender and let stand for 1 hour. The lavender sugar keeps for only two weeks before the moisture in the lavender causes lumping, which makes the sugar difficult to sieve.

Serves 4 to 6

Researchers have found that men are aroused more by the smell of lavender and pumpkin together than any other tested fragrance. Whatever the fragrances' impact may be, this is a *very* good-tasting, moist, rich dessert. It is wonderful after a repast where the entree features lavender as a spice. The dairy and citrus help bring out the best of the lavender flavor and aroma. The pudding was developed by Kandis Kozolanka.

For the pudding:
  ½ cup unsalted butter
  6 tablespoons granulated sugar
  6 tablespoons brown sugar
  1 egg
  1 cup all-purpose flour
  1 teaspoon ground cinnamon
  1 teaspoon salt
  1¾ teaspoons baking soda
  ¼ cup milk
  ¼ cup orange juice
  2 to 5 ounces pureed pumpkin
  1 teaspoon vanilla extract
  Lavender flowers and leaves for garnish

Lavender whipped cream:
  1 cup heavy cream
  2 tablespoons sugar
  3 tablespoons finely ground, chopped fresh
    lavender flowers

To make the pudding, in a medium bowl, beat the butter and sugars together until fluffy. Add the egg and blend.

In another medium bowl, sift the flour, cinnamon, salt, and baking soda together. Add the dry ingredi-ents alternately with the milk and the juice to the butter mixture, beginning and ending with the flour mixture. Fold in the pureed pumpkin and vanilla, blending well.

Butter a 1-quart mold. Add the pudding and cover with parchment paper, then with aluminum foil. Place the mold in a large saucepan. Fill the saucepan with hot water so that it comes halfway up the sides of the mold. Cover the saucepan, place over low heat, and steam very slowly for 2 ½ hours.

Remove the mold from the water and set on rack. When the mold is lukewarm, turn it upside down on a plate. The pudding should slide out easily.

To make the whipped cream, place the cream in a bowl, and, using a wire whisk, whip until it starts to hold a soft peak. Add the sugar and lavender flowers.

To assemble the pudding, cut it horizontally into three to five layers, depending on the depth of the mold used. The more layers in the dessert, the better the pumpkin and lavender flavors will marry. Drop a dollop of cream onto the bottom layer and lay the next pudding layer lightly on top of the cream. Repeat with each layer. Cover the top with cream, and garnish with whole lavender flowers and leaves.

Farms and Gardens

To see local examples of lavender species, first visit the yellow pages and look for the following:

- Arboretums and botanical gardens.
- Retail nurseries that maintain demonstration plantings.
- Garden clubs that care for demonstration plantings.
- Plant societies or groups such as native plant societies (members may be growing lavender even though it's not a native), regional horticultural groups, Xeriscape organizations, or landscaper contractor associations.

Lavender is very drought resistant, and some water districts have planted water-conserving gardens as models for drought-tolerant landscaping. Similarly, some fire districts have planting demonstrations of fire-retardent or fire-safe landscaping—lavender fits in this category as well.

Here are some regional places where lavender is grown on a large scale and gardens are open to the public:

Barbara's Lavender Farm
1355 Spruston Rd.
Cassidy, BC
Canada
(250) 245-8196

MAILING ADDRESS
PO Box 964
Nanaimo, BC V9R 5N2
Canada

E-MAIL
gschulz@islandnet.com
WEB PAGE
http:// www.ibnd.com/
lavender.html

Cape Cod Lavender Farm
Iland Pond Trail
Harwitch Center, MA 02645
(508) 432-8977

MAILING ADDRESS
PO Box 611
Harwitch Center, MA 02645

E-MAIL
cclafarm@capecod.net
WEB PAGE
http://www.capecod.net/
lavender

Happy Valley Herb Farm
3497 Happy Valley Road
Victoria, BC V9C 2Y2
Canada
(250) 474-5767

*Matanzas Creek Winery and
Estate Grown Lavender*
6097 Bennett Valley Rd.
Santa Rosa, CA 95404
(707) 528-6464

E-MAIL
matcrkwine@aol.com
WEB PAGE
http://www.
matanzascreek.com

Seeds and Plants

Carrol Gardens
PO Box 310
444 E. Main St.
Westminster, MD 21158

Companion Plants
7247 N. Coolville Ridge Rd.
Athens, OH 45701

Cornflower Farms, Inc.
PO Box 896
Elk Grove, CA 95759

Digging Dog Nursery
PO Box 471
Albion, CA 95410

Fedco Seeds
52 Mayflower Hill Drive
Waterville, ME 04901

Foothill Cottage Gardens
13925 Sontag Rd.
Grass Valley, CA 95945

Goodwin Creek Gardens
PO Box 83
Williams, OR 97544

It's About Thyme
11726 Manchaca Rd.
Austin, TX 78748

J. L. Hudson, Seedsman
PO Box 1058
Redwood City, CA 94064

Le Jardin du Gourmet
PO Box 75
St. Johnsbury Center, VT 05863

Meadowbrook Herb Garden
93 Kingstown Rd.
Wyoming, RI 02898

Merry Gardens
PO Box 595
Mechanic Street
Camden, ME 04843

Mountain Valley Growers
38325 Pepperweed Rd.
Squaw Valley, CA 93675

Nichols Garden Nursery, Inc.
1190 North Pacific Highway
Albany, OR 97321-4598

Rasland Farm
NC 82 at US 13
Godwin, NC 28344-9712

Richters Herbs
357 Highway 47
Goodwood, Ontario L0C 1A0
Canada

The Rosemary House
120 South Market St.
Mechanicsburg, PA 17055

Sandy Mush Herb Nursery
Route 2, Surett Cove Rd.
Leicester, NC 28748

Shepherd's Garden Seeds
30 Irene St.
Torrington, CT 06790

Sleepy Hollow Herb Farm
568 Jack Black Rd.
Lancaster, KY 40444-9306

Smith & Hawken
Two Arbor Lane
Box 6900
Florence, KY 41022-6900

Stokes Seeds Inc.
PO Box 548
Buffalo, NY 14240

T. DeBaggio Herbs
923 N. Ivy St.
Arlington, VA 22201

Territorial Seed Company
PO Box 157
Cottage Grove, OR 97424

Thompson & Morgan Inc.
PO Box 1308
Jackson, NJ 08527-0308

Well-Sweep Herb Farm
317 Mt. Bethel Road
Port Murray, NJ 07865

Wrenwood of Berkeley Springs
Route 4, Box 361
Berkeley Springs, WV 24511

Businesses that cater to the growing interest in aromatherapy are good places to buy high-quality essential lavender oils. Here's a brief listing put together, in great part, by the International Aromatherapy and Herb Association, 3541 West Acapulco Lane, Phoenix, Arizona 85023; (602) 938-4439; E-mail: jeffreys@aztec.asu.edu.

A Woman of Uncommon Scents
PO Box 103
Roxbury, PA 17251
(800) 377-3685
(717) 530-0609
FAX (717) 263-6347
E-MAIL 75730.1510@compuserve.com

Aroma Therapy International
3319 River Pines
Ann Arbor, MI 48103
(313) 741-1617
E-MAIL eurolink@umich.edu

Aroma Vera
5901 Rodeo Rd.
Los Angeles, CA 90016-4312
(800) 669-9514
(310) 280-0407
FAX (310) 280-0395

Aromatherapy Hut
8628 W. Davis Rd.
Peoria, AZ 85382
(602) 974-6065
FAX (602) 876-1331

Aromatic Osmosis
502 Queen St. W
Toronto, Ontario M5V 3B2
Canada
(800) IRISES-5
(416) 703-6166
FAX (416) 703-6162
E-MAIL osmosisoil@aol.com

Essential Oil Company
PO Box 206
Lake Oswego, OR 97034
(800) 729-5912
(503) 697-5992
FAX (503) 697-0615
E-MAIL essentialoil@essentialoil.com

Essentially Oils
8 Mount Farm, Junction Rd.
Churchill, Chipping Norton
Oxfordshire 0X7 6NP
England
011-44-1608 659544
E-MAIL essentially.oils.ltd@dial.pipex.com

Healthware 2 Bodycare
  610 22 St., ste. 247
  San Francisco, CA 94107
  (800) 829-6580
  (415) 626-7378
  F A X (415) 626-7803

The Herb Store
  107 Carlisle SE
  Albuquerque, NM 87107
  (800) 203-3504
  (505) 255-1333
  F A X (505) 255-7901

Legendary Ethnobotanical Resources
  16245 SW 304th St.
  Homestead, FL 33033
  (305) 242-0877

Moonrise Herbs
  826 G St.
  Arcata, CA 95521
  (707) 822-5296
  F A X (707) 822-0506
  E - M A I L moonrise@botanical.com

Mountain Rose Herbs
  PO Box 2000
  Redway, CA 95560
  (800) 879-3337

RJF, Inc.
  32422 Alipaz, ste. C
  San Juan Capistrano, CA 92675
  (800) 933-1008
  (714) 240-1104
  F A X (714) 489-4384

Timeless Apothecary
  A Division of Atwood Institute
  6845 W. McKnight Loop
  Glendale, AZ 85308
  (800) 642-9339
  (602) 547-9174
  F A X (602) 978-8224
  E - M A I L hypnosis@primenet.com

Wild Weeds
  PO Box 88
  Ferndale, CA 95536
  (800) 553-9453
  (707) 786-4906
  F A X (800) 836-9453

This map loosely defines the range of average annual minimum temperatures for each zone in degrees F (NOTE: zones 1, 2, and 11 are outside the continental United States). Contact your local garden center for more specific information about your particular climate.

Zone	1	Below –50°	Zone	7	0° to 10°
	2	–50° to –40°		8	10° to 20°
	3	–40° to –30°		9	20° to 30°
	4	–30° to –20°		10	30° to 40°
	5	–20° to –10°		11	40° and above
	6	–10° to 0°			

Index

ACKNOWLEDGMENTS

Thanks to the following dear friends for their support during this project: Chester Aaron, Ron & Patsy Chamberlain, Michael Eschenbach and Salli Rasberry, Mimi Luebbermann, Myra Portwood, "Sooz" Reeder, Jim Sullivan and Linda Parker, Clayton Ward and Marshia Loar, and Patricia Winters.

I also want to thank the following professionals and stellar chefs who gave special advice and technical input above and beyond the call of duty: Suzanne Adams, Caterer, Occidental, CA; Mandy Aftel, Grandiflora Perfumes, Berkeley, CA; Barbara Barton, author of *Gardening by Mail,* Sebastopol, CA; Coralie Castle, author, San Rafael, CA; Jan "The-Lovely-Lady-of-the-Lavender" Coello, Matanzas Creek Winery & Estate Lavender, Santa Rosa, CA; Ditty Deamer, Ditty's Saturday Market Web site, San Francisco, CA; Dick Dunmire, semi-retired former editor for *Sunset* magazine; Tamara Frey, chef, Frey Winery, Redwood Valley, CA; Amie Hill, Editor, Occidental, CA; Cy Hyde, Well-Sweep Herbs, Port Murray, NJ; Kandis Kozolanka, Caterer, Occidental, CA; Mimi Luebbermann, Author, Farmer, Chef, Caterer, and Pond Builder, Petaluma, CA; John Mancarella, owner, The Belmont, Belmont, MA; Tess McDonough, chef, Kendall Jackson Winery, Santa Rosa, CA; Nora Pouillon, chef, Restaurant Nora, Washington, D.C.; Jerry Traunfeld, chef, The Herbfarm, Fall City, WA; Maggie Wych, Western Hills Nursery, Occidental, CA; Barbara Schulz, Barbara's Lavender Farm, British Columbia; and Cynthia Sutphin, Cape Cod Lavender Farm, Harwich Port, MA. Special thanks to Gary Ratway and Deborah Wigham of Diggery Dog Nursey for help double-checking named variety lavenders.

Thanks to Joy Larkcom, part of my informal writer's support group—by fax all the way from England. A source of inspiration. She also loaned me her copy of *The Story of Lavender* by Sally Festing—which provided many of the cute poems and lavender hawker's cries.

Very special appreciation goes to Dr. Arthur O. Tucker, Research Professor at the University of Delaware, Department of Agriculture and Natural Resources, Dover, DE, and Tom DeBaggio, owner of T. DeBaggio Herbs in Arlington, VA. Together, these are the best lavender minds (and hands) in the country. They provided invaluable feedback to key portions of the manuscript. Thanks.

Martha Cassleman, my agent, for making all this possible and for being such a supportive help when things got turbulent or sluggish. Thanks to the folks at Chronicle Books: Leslie Jonath, Sarah Putman, and Jill Jacobson as well as Judith Dunham and Deborah Jones—this certainly was the easiest book to write in my entire career.